The Dynamic World 3

———— MANAGEMENT ————
WATER . ENVIRONMENT . ENERGY

M. J. READMAN
Headteacher, The Clough Hall School, Kidsgrove

F. M. MAYERS
Headteacher, The Pingle School, Swadlincote

OLIVER & BOYD

Acknowledgements

The publishers thank the following for permission to reproduce photographs or other copyright material:

Mark Edwards/Still Pictures (1.3a, 2.27); Tony Waltham (1.3b, 2.14, 2.30, 2.34, 2.44, 5.15, 7.11, 9.2, 9.4, 10.2, 16.8); ICCE/Rose Winnall (1.3c); J. Allan Cash (1.3d, 2.6, 2.13, 2.40, 5.4a, 5.5, 7.8, 7.10, 9.3, 9.7c, 10.1, 11.4, 11.13a, 12.3, 13.11, 14.8, 16.5, 17.3); Balfour Maunsell Ltd (2.21a,b); Christian Aid (2.28); Thames Water plc (2.29, 2.38); Miele (2.31); *Leek Post and Times* (2.43); *Stoke Evening Sentinel* (2.44); Greg O'Hare (4.1); ODA (4.4a–e); Eric Kay (4.6); Soil Association (4.9); Tony and Marion Morrison (5.3a, 5.6); World Wide Fund for Nature (5.12 photo: Claudio Marigo, 8.1 map); *The Independent* (5.12 text); Clive Carter (5.14a,b); The Woodland Trust (5.18); Panos (6.2 Jeremy Hartley, Oxfam, 12.2 Ron Giling, 18.5b Herbert Girardet, 18.16 David Reed); F. M. Mayers (7.4, 7.5, 7.6, 7.7); Today Newspapers Ltd (7.12 text and photos, 11.11 text and photo 11.11a); Heather Angel (8.1 top & bottom left); Maurice Nimmo (8.1 top right); Nature Conservancy Council/Richard Lindsay (8.1 bottom right); Nature Photographers Ltd (8.2); Charlotte Deane (11.13b); Photo Co-op/Santiago Castrillon (9.7a,b); National Water Sports Centre (10.4); The Environmental Picture Library/M. Bond (11.5); Greenpeace (11.11b, 19.1); Barnaby's Picture Library (11.12); Aluminium Can Recycling Association (11.13c); National Power (12.7); British Coal (13.4, 13.9); ZEFA (13.5); Richard and Sally Greenhill (13.6); BP (14.7, 14.10); Rex Features (14.13, 15.8); UK Atomic Energy Authority (15.2); Dr Shirin Akiner (6.5); Documentation Française (16.6); P. Morris (16.10); Topham (18.5a); Brian & Cherry Alexander/Paul Drummond (18.17); Greenpeace/Friends of the Earth (19.1); Sainsbury's (19.2); Prudential/BTCV (19.3); BBC (19.4).

Cover photographs by Tony Waltham (2) and J. Allan Cash

The authors would like to acknowledge the following sources which were used as a basis for figures or text:

David Jones, Environmental Editor, *Today* (Isle of Wight text, p. 6); Gemini News Service GSC 227 (Zimbabwe text, p. 12); A. Horsfield, 'A Senegal Village Water Supply Project', *Journal of the Institute of Water and Environmental Management*, August 1988 (Senegal text, pp. 12–13; 2.19, 2.20); Gemini News Service GG 69554 (Tegucigalpas text, p. 15); Christian Aid (2.28); *Financial Times* 23 June 1986 (2.37); OECD and *Financial Times* (2.41); AA/Readers Digest, *Book of the British Countryside* (3.3); Kirby and Morgan, *Soil Erosion*, John Wiley 1980 (4.7); Evans and Nortcliff, *Journal of Agricultural Science*, vol. 90, 1978 (4.8); Soil Association (4.9); Earthlife (Cameroon text, p. 31); Gemini News Service GSC 274, 1989 (Agro-forestry text, p. 31); Nature Conservancy Council Data Support for Education sheet 5 (5.16, 5.17); The Woodland Trust (5.18); Charles Tyler, The Arid Earth, *Geographical Magazine*, May 1989 (6.1 and related text); ITV series 'Climate and Man' (text pp. 34–5); Goldsmith and Hildyard, *The Earth Report*, Mitchell Beazley (6.4 and related text, 18.2, 18.18, text pp. 56, 71, 72–3, 74–5, 78–9); Teignbridge District Council Planning Department (7.3 and text on Dawlish Warren Nature Reserve); Nature Conservancy Council, 'Sand Dunes: a Coastal Landform with Economic Value' (sand dune text, p. 37); *Today*, 8 August 1989 (On the Brink text, p. 38); World Wide Fund for Nature, 'Wetlands in Danger' (8.3); Jamie Skinner, 'Lake in the Desert', *Birds* (RSPB), Autumn 1985 (Lake Ichkeul text); Department of the Environment, 'Evaluating Derelict Land Grant Schemes', 1987 (9.5); *Geofile*, April 1988 (9.6); Welsh Development Agency, 'Working with Nature', June 1987 (9.10); London Waste Regulation Authority (11.3a–c); Packington Estate Enterprise Ltd and *Geofile*, January 1989 (11.8); Glass Manufacturers Federation (11.15); *BP Statistical Review of World Energy* (12.1, 12.4, 12.5, 12.6, 13.1, 13.2, 14.1, 14.2, 14.3, 14.4a, 14.5, 14.9); National Power (12.8, 12.9, 12.10); *Geofile*, April 1988 (13.3, 13.7); British Coal Corporation and *Geofile*, January 1988 (text pp. 60–1); 'British Coal Report and Accounts', 1988 (13.8); British Gas (14.6); 'Sullom Voe', Sullom Voe Oil Terminal (text p. 66); *Today*, 28 and 29 March 1989 (text on p. 67, 14.14, 14.15, 14.16); Shell UK (14.12); British Nuclear Fuels, 'Sellafield Visitors Centre – A Window on the Nuclear World' (15.1); P. M. S. Jones, *Energy and the Need for Nuclear Power*, United Kingdom Atomic Energy Authority (15.3); UKAEA (15.5, 15.6); Council for Education in World Citizenship, 'The Outlook for Nuclear Power in The Shadow of Chernobyl' (text p. 71); 'Severn Wonder of the World', *Today*, 24 October 1989 (16.4); Susan Gubbay, 'The Cost of Tidal Power', *Marine Conservation*, Summer 1987 (text p. 73); The Electricity Council (text p. 74); 'Harnessing the Wind', *Geographical Magazine*, June 1989 (text p. 75); British Power, 'Power from the Wind' (16.9 and related text);

John Seymour and Herbert Girardet, *Blueprint for a Green Planet*, Dorling Kindersley (16.7, 16.14, 16.15, 18.11, 18.12, 18.13, 18.14 and text pp. 86–7); 'Sugar: The Fuel of the Future', *The Observer*, 9 February 1986 (16.11 and related text); 'Dustbin Power', The Warmer Campaign (16.13); The Association for the Conservation of Energy (text pp. 76–7); E. Broadley and R. Goring, *Studies in Geography 2*, Oliver & Boyd (17.2); Greenpeace Environmental Trust, 'Eight Ways the North Sea is being Poisoned' (17.5); World Wide Fund for Nature, 'Nature Watch' (17.6), 'Acid Rain and Air Pollution' (18.1, 18.4); Watch Trust for Environmental Education, 'Acid Drops' (18.2); Friends of the Earth, 'Acid Rain' (18.3); 'The Very Air', *The Economist*, 16 May 1987, and Greenpeace 'The Acid Rain Tragedy' (text pp. 82–3); 'The Greenhouse Effect', *New Scientist*, 22 October 1988 (18.6); J. F. B. Mitchell, *The Greenhouse Effect and Climate Change*, Meteorological Office (18.8); Ark Trust (18.9); World Wide Fund for Nature, newsletter no. 2, 1989: 'A Program to Save the African Elephant' (text p. 88); Greenpeace, 'Antarctica' (text p. 89).

Illustrations 2.2, 5.11, 15.7, 15.10 and 18.15 were supplied by Gemini News Service, London (Tel. 071 833 4141); illustrations 1.1, 2.11, 2.17, 11.10, 14.4b, 16.12, 17.1, 17.4, 18.7, 18.10 and 19.5 are based on Gemini illustrations.

Designed and typeset by Oxprint Ltd, Oxford.
Illustrated by Swanston Graphics Ltd, Derby.

Oliver & Boyd
Longman House
Burnt Mill
Harlow
Essex CM20 2JE
An Imprint of the Longman Group UK Ltd

ISBN 0 05 004366 8
First published 1991
Third impression 1994

© Oliver & Boyd 1991. All rights reserved; no part of this publication may be reproduced, stored in a retrieval system, or transmitted in any form or by any means, electronic, mechanical, photocopying, recording or otherwise, without either the prior written permission of the publishers or a licence permitting restricted copying in the United Kingdom issued by the Copyright Licensing Agency Ltd, 90 Tottenham Court Road, London, W1P 9HE.

Typeset in $9\frac{1}{2}$/11pt Palatino

Printed in Hong Kong
CTPS/03

Contents

		Page
1	Looking after the Earth	4
2	Water	6
3	Understanding Ecosystems	22
4	Soil	24
5	Forest Ecosystems	28
6	Desertification	34
7	Coastal Management	36
8	Wetlands	40
9	The Need for Land	42
10	Quarrying	46
11	Rubbish?	48
12	Energy	54
13	Coal	58
14	Oil and Natural Gas	62
15	Nuclear Power	68
16	Fuels of the Future?	72
17	Managing the Oceans	78
18	Environmental Decisions	82
19	Who Cares?	90
Glossary		94
Index		96

1 Looking after the Earth

Key ideas
- The earth faces many threats to life, land, sea and air.
- We are increasingly aware of these threats, understand more about them and, as a result, are taking positive steps to reduce their impact.

The earth has traditionally been seen as a limitless store of materials to be used by people without any real concern. With rising world population and improved technology, ever-increasing demands are being made on the world's resources (e.g. energy supplies) and on its basic life-supporting systems (e.g. the atmosphere and oceans). The late twentieth century has seen much more awareness of the problems caused by these demands. Unfortunately this has come too late to prevent a great deal of permanent damage. 1.1 shows the scale and variety of some of the major threats to the earth.

Much greater understanding is still needed about the consequences of our misuse of the earth. However, the present more responsible attitude by an increasing number of people offers real hope for the future.

Resources: How Long Will They Last?

A whole range of **resources** is needed to support modern life. These include the air we breathe, the water we use in a wide variety of ways, and the soil in which we grow food. Also important are such things as timber, rocks, minerals and energy supplies.

▼ 1.1 The threats to the earth

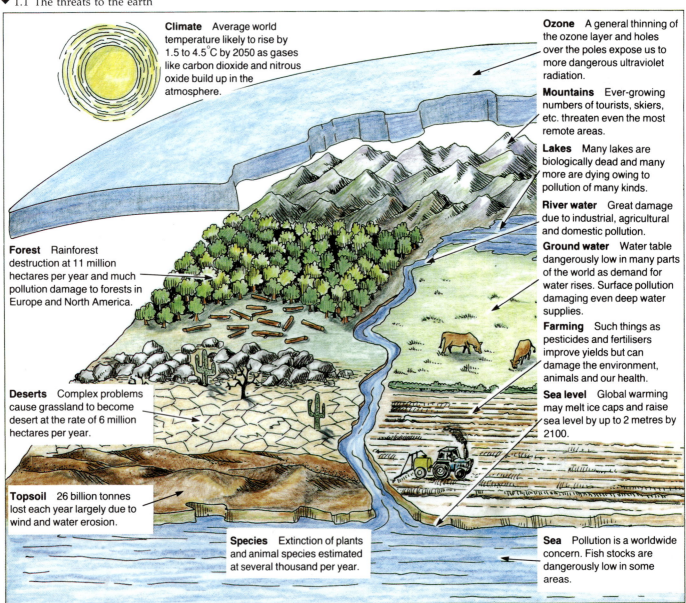

Some resources are **non-renewable** or **finite**; once used up they cannot be replaced. Others are **renewable** or **non-finite** and with careful management will last forever. Table 1.2 gives information about some resources and their uses. *Make up a list of (a) renewable and (b) non-renewable resources.*

Some non-renewable materials are running out and great care must be taken to make them last as long as possible. The **recycling** of metals and more efficient conversion of coal to electricity are two examples of how this can be done.

To maintain renewable resources the rate of use must balance the rate of renewal. Great care must be taken to resist the temptation of a short-term profit resulting in current supplies being used up at a faster rate than they can be replaced.

Resource	Uses
Soil	Plant growth, basis of agriculture
Coal, oil, natural gas	Fuel and power; raw materials for industry
Water	Life support, agriculture, raw material for industry
Timber	Building, furniture, paper and chemicals
Metal ores	Metal working: enormous variety of industrial uses
Sand, gravel	Building and construction
Air	Life support

▲ 1.2 Some resources and their uses

◀ Land   ▶ Rivers

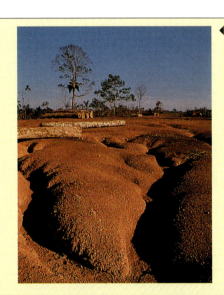

THE FUTURE?

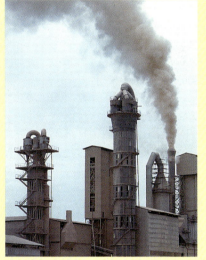

◀ Sea   ▶ Air

▲ 1.3 The future?

The Future

Some non-renewable resources in short supply can be replaced with alternative renewable ones. For example ethanol from sugar cane (an annually renewable crop) can replace petrol which is derived from non-renewable oil.

Many people believe that it is the basic life-support systems of the earth that face the greatest threats now and in the future. 1.3 shows how four of these systems are currently threatened. We have the technology to solve most of the problems shown but often considerable financial cost is involved. However, many people think the environmental cost of the damage being done far outweighs the financial costs of solving such problems.

For each photograph in 1.3 describe the environmental cost of what is shown and outline what you think should be done about the situation.

Looking after the Earth 5

2 Water

Key ideas
- Water is a renewable resource often taken for granted in developed countries.
- The hydrological cycle must be understood if proper water management is to take place.

Water: The Vital Resource

In developed countries such as the United Kingdom, increasingly large amounts of water are used (2.1). Future demand is likely to rise still further as appliances such as dishwashers and waste disposal units become more common. Not only must all this water be supplied but it must also be safely treated after use. With this in mind, the Water Authorities Association (WAA) are attempting to change the public's attitude. They are trying to get the public to understand that, although water is a renewable resource, supplies are not *infinite* and it becomes increasingly costly to supply as demand rises.

Look at the article on water metering and explain how the WAA are trying to change people's attitudes. Do you think it will work?

2.2 gives some information about water supply on a world scale. Notice two major problems:

- how little of the world's water is available for human use;
- millions of people lack a proper water supply and sanitation.

The second problem is highlighted by a World Health Organisation report which states that each person needs 70 litres of water per day for a reasonable quality of life. In the USA the amount used is 300 litres per day but in India it is just 25 litres per day.

The water cycle

On a world scale water continually circulates between land, air and ocean. Water evaporates from land and sea surfaces as water vapour and then condenses to form cloud and rain which returns to the earth's

▼ 2.1

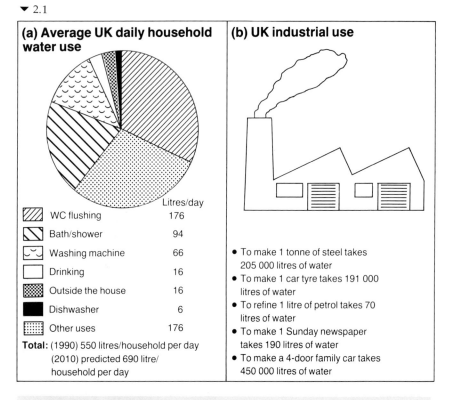

(a) Average UK daily household water use

	Litres/day
WC flushing	176
Bath/shower	94
Washing machine	66
Drinking	16
Outside the house	16
Dishwasher	6
Other uses	176

Total: (1990) 550 litres/household per day
(2010) predicted 690 litre/household per day

(b) UK industrial use

- To make 1 tonne of steel takes 205 000 litres of water
- To make 1 car tyre takes 191 000 litres of water
- To refine 1 litre of petrol takes 70 litres of water
- To make 1 Sunday newspaper takes 190 litres of water
- To make a 4-door family car takes 450 000 litres of water

Water metering in the Isle of Wight

Did you soak in a relaxing bath filled to the brim this morning, or take a shower? Do you use a mugful of water when brushing your teeth, or let the tap run? The differences might seem trivial but they do cost money. As we begin to realise that there is not a never-ending supply of cheap water our attitudes must change. On 1 April 1989 the first metering scheme went on trial in the Isle of Wight. There were also test runs in nine smaller areas from Yorkshire to Dorset. On the Isle of Wight water will cost about 28p per 1000 litres for the first 90 000 litres, rising sharply to 53p per 1000 litres after that. So on the higher charge band the average bath will cost 4.3p whereas a shower would cost only 1.9p. 'People generally think it is much fairer' said spokeswoman Sally Webb. 'They will have to think twice about leaving that garden hose running for hours during the summer, but they will actually be able to control what they spend on water, as people do in almost every other country.'

Meters are unlikely to become widespread in the UK before the mid 1990s. The pilot schemes will be assessed after three years and the time taken to install meters in every house will be considerable.

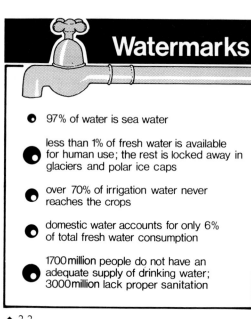

Watermarks

- 97% of water is sea water
- less than 1% of fresh water is available for human use; the rest is locked away in glaciers and polar ice caps
- over 70% of irrigation water never reaches the crops
- domestic water accounts for only 6% of total fresh water consumption
- 1700 million people do not have an adequate supply of drinking water; 3000 million lack proper sanitation

▲ 2.2

surface. This system is called the **water cycle** or **hydrological cycle**. The land part of this cycle is most important to understand if water supply is to be managed properly. 2.3a shows the **drainage basin** hydrological cycle as a block diagram, and 2.3b shows it as a system diagram. A drainage basin is the area around a river. It supplies water to a network of drainage channels and is usually named after the main river of the basin. The drainage basin is the major unit of land for water supply management. Within a drainage basin it is possible to do a number of things to make more water available for use. These include

- building a dam across a river channel to increase surface storage,
- changing the vegetation cover to reduce evaporation and transpiration,
- adopting farming practices which encourage infiltration rather than allowing the water to run straight off the surface.

▼ 2.3 The hydrological cycle

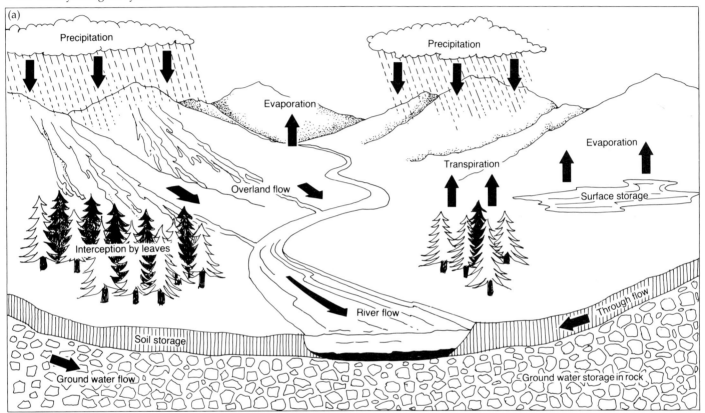

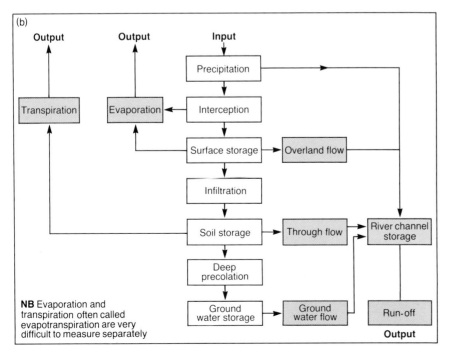

▼ 2.4 Key terms in the hydrological cycle

Precipitation	Rain, drizzle, sleet, snow and dew
Interception	Precipitation trapped by vegetation before it reaches the ground
Infiltration	Water moving into soil.
Evaporation	Water lost as vapour from earth's surface to the atmosphere
Transpiration	Water taken in from soil by plant roots which moves to the leaves and is lost by evaporation to the atmosphere via pores.
Run-off	All the water left to enter rivers after evaporation and transpiration have occurred. It includes overland flow, throughflow and ground water flow.
Storage	Water stored in different parts of the drainage basin.
Percolation	Movement of water through rock or soil.

Managing the resource

There are three natural **stores** of water within the hydrological cycle: rivers, lakes, and underground (2.5). These stores may be large or small and may be increased artificially by such things as dam building. If supplies of water are to be managed properly the **yield** of the stores (both natural and artificial) must be calculated and matched against the demand from the various uses of water (2.5). The **reliable yield** is the amount that can be **abstracted** (taken) in times of *lowest* rainfall; whether that happens regularly in a particular season, or is likely to occur only once within a period of say 10 years. It is the guaranteed minimum supply and is therefore used in all calculations. Predicted future demand must be considered so that any necessary artificial increase can be planned well in advance.

There is also great concern about what happens to the water after it has been used (2.5). One answer is simply to put it into rivers or the sea in an untreated form. However, this can cause pollution, sometimes to a dangerous level, and it can cause waterborne diseases. In some cases, untreated water may be dumped into a river at a point in its course, then abstracted again lower down. Sewage and water treatment works are an accepted part of water management in many developed areas of the world, but they are extremely expensive to build and operate, and more are needed in many developed and in most developing areas.

▼ 2.5 Water stores, uses and treatment

New demands on water

As an area develops, new industry and increased wealth push up the demand for water. The increased wealth also brings more demand for sport and recreation, and this can mean rivers, lakes and reservoirs become used as centres for watersports and fishing (2.6). The land around reservoirs and the shallow-water margins of reservoirs are important habitats for many sorts of wildlife and these also attract many visitors. Maintaining water levels, water quality and allowing (often conflicting) recreational users access to water is becoming an increasingly important part of water management.

◀ 2.6 Leisure use of water

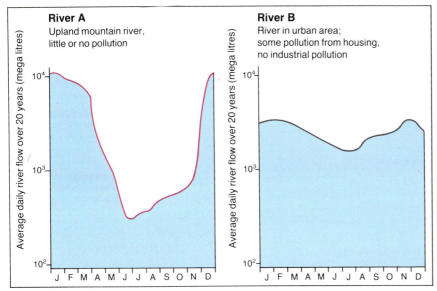

▲ 2.7 River hydrographs

Natural factors
- Deep valley to allow easier dam construction
- Impermeable rock to prevent loss of water into ground beneath
- More precipitation than evapotranspiration
- Suitable vegetation cover on hillsides to prevent excess soil washing down into reservoir

Human factors
- Low population density to minimise settlement flooding
- Poor agricultural land e.g. land for extensive sheep grazing
- Local people willing to adapt to new ways of making a living, e.g. offering facilities to visitors

▲ 2.8 Suitable factors for building a reservoir

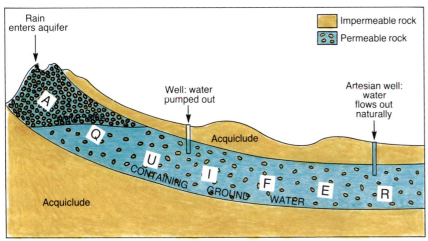

▲ 2.9 An aquifer

Water from a river?

Water abstracted from a river may go directly into the supply system, after treatment to make it fit to drink. Often it is first pumped into artificial storage reservoirs which make water available in times of low river flow. The reservoirs are replenished during periods of higher flow.

The river's flow rate is measured for a number of years to obtain an accurate picture of the average reliable yield. The results can then be shown on a **hydrograph** (2.7). *Study the two hydrographs in 2.7 and the information about each river. Assume the need is to abstract the maximum amount of water of drinking quality to meet a demand that varies little throughout the year. State the advantages and disadvantages of each river and suggest what could be done to overcome the disadvantages.*

Water from a reservoir?

Precipitation levels are generally high in many upland and mountain areas. Here soils are usually thin, and rapid surface run-off of water takes place. If a dam can be built across a narrow part of a valley, the water that would quickly run into the sea can be stored for use. 2.8 shows some of the natural and human factors needed for an area to be ideally suitable for dam construction. Big dam construction is very costly but vast volumes of water can be stored, allowing extensive irrigation and in some cases the generation of hydro-electric power.

Sometimes local people are against the building of a reservoir in their area. They resent having to change their way of life so that people in a distant part of the country who need water may benefit. *How can such conflicts be kept to a minimum?*

Water from underground?

Rocks such as chalk, limestone, sandstone or sand and gravel beds are called **aquifers** (2.9). Aquifers are water-bearing rocks from which water can be abstracted because the rocks are **permeable**. This means the rocks have cracks or pores which store water and which are also large enough to let water pass through the rock. Where the aquifer reaches the surface, rain water easily enters the rock and becomes known as **ground water** (see page 7). Sometimes an aquifer is sandwiched between two layers of **impermeable** rock called **acquicludes**. Water trapped in such an aquifer can build up pressure and, if a bore hole is made through the upper acquiclude, water will flow to the surface under its own pressure. When this happens it is called an **artesian** bore hole. Underground water is often very pure and requires minimal treatment before drinking. *Why must careful records be kept of the amount of water abstracted from bore holes?*

Water 9

Key idea
- The provision of adequate drinking water and sanitation to people in developing areas is one of the greatest challenges facing the world.

Water: Developing Countries

Half of the world's hospital beds are occupied by people with water-related diseases.

For a poor family in urban Sudan the price paid for water may be as high as 15% of the household income. In Britain an average family's daily water bill is less than the cost of a pint of milk.

According to the National Environment Engineering Research Institute in Bombay, 70% of India's inland water is unfit for human consumption.

The number of water taps per person is a better indication of health than the number of hospital beds.

In the Sudan the introduction of wells, pumps and water distribution points saves the women an average of 6 hours work a day.

In Burkina Faso in Africa some women walk 2–3 hours every day to get water. They carry back 25 kilograms of water. This trip uses 600 calories per day; one-third of the daily food intake.

Diarrhoea among children under 5 in a group of villages in India plunged from 84 per thousand to just 19 per thousand in 3 years following the installation of a safe water supply.

The tap is the centre of attraction in many villages in Nepal; it brings progress and the hope of a better life for the future.

To be able to wash is a luxury and a joy that should be available to everyone. Not only does it give a sense of comfort but most importantly it enables people to stay in good health.

▲ 2.10

▼ 2.12 Water and sanitation

- 80% of diseases in developing areas are transmitted by dirty water
- Diarrhoea alone kills 6 million children each year

Malaria, river blindness, parasitic worms: transmitted by water-breeding insects

Eye diseases, scabies, leprosy: transmitted by contact with unclean water

Typhoid, cholera, dysentery, diarrhoea: transmitted by drinking or washing in contaminated water

Hookworm: transmitted by poor sanitation

▲ 2.11 Deadly water

1981–1990 was the United Nations International Drinking Water Supply and Sanitation decade. Many projects and schemes were set up in developing areas to improve the quality of drinking water and to introduce or improve sanitation. 2.10 gives some information about the water supply and sanitation problems facing many developing countries, and offers examples of hopeful signs for the future. 2.11 describes some of the many diseases that can result from unclean water. During the UN decade many billions of pounds were spent and much was achieved. Governments in developed and developing countries worked together, and with voluntary aid organisations, on thousands of projects, both large and small. As a result, the percentage of people with safe drinking water and adequate sanitation increased. However, because of population increase during the decade, the total number of people without safe water remained about the same, while the number without sanitation increased by over 100 million. Also the majority of the money was spent on improving conditions in urban areas of developing countries, whereas the problem is most serious in rural areas (2.12).

Urban problems

2.13 shows people from a **shanty town** on the outskirts of Brasilia collecting water. *Describe fully what the picture shows and list reasons why this water supply is likely to be unsafe to drink.* Shanty towns are largely unplanned settlements of self-built

▼ 2.13 Brasilia

▶ 2.14 Java

▼ 2.15

makeshift houses. They grow rapidly as people with little or no money arrive in an urban area looking for work. Many of these people come from surrounding rural areas. The authorities often cannot cope with the influx and it may be many years before even water standpipes become available.

The problems can be lessened if the authorities decide in advance where the next shanty town should be. Then simple building materials are made available at affordable prices and, most importantly, water and sewerage systems are installed before any building starts.

Rural problems

In most developing countries, problems of water supply and sanitation are very severe in rural areas (2.12). 2.14 shows a typical scene at a waterhole in Java. People and cattle share the same water. *Can you explain why conditions are especially dangerous if the water supply is a seasonally filled pond rather than a river or stream?* The need to separate human from animal use is obvious **but** costly. The rural population have little or no money to bring about change and governments often give priority to trying to solve problems in urban areas.

Water is development

Most experts agree that safe water and good health are a basis for development. Whatever schemes are adopted to improve water and sanitation, three fundamental things must be central to them.

1 *Appropriate technology*. Equipment which is simple to install, operate and maintain is essential. *Look at 2.15 and describe the message of the cartoon. Do you think this is an effective way of putting over the message?*
2 *Local community involvement*. The local people must feel part of the scheme. This will encourage them to accept responsibility for it. It is especially important that women are fully involved.
3 *Education and training*. This helps local people to understand the need for improved sanitation and how to use and maintain equipment to ensure a trouble-free supply of clean water. General hygiene education must also be provided if the health of a community is to improve significantly.

If water and sanitation are improved then other long-term improvements follow:

- disease and infant mortality rates are lowered,
- productivity increases,
- living standards are raised.

Together these can lead to an upturn in the economy of a developing country.

Water

▲ 2.16 Location of Zimbabwe

▼ 2.18 Location of Senegal

▼ 2.17 Simple technology

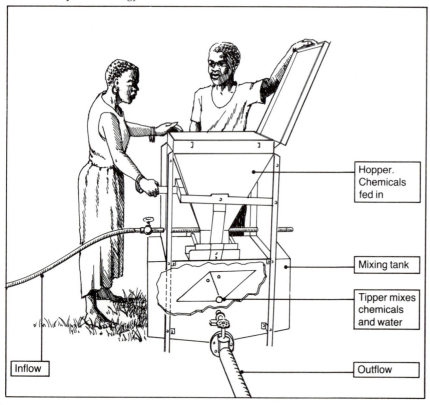

Zimbabwe discovers small is beautiful

Zimbabwe (2.16), like many other developing countries, has found that over-ambitious development schemes, often suggested by outside advisors, can have serious drawbacks including:

- high initial cost,
- high running costs for such things as fuel and spare parts,
- the need for highly trained people to operate and maintain equipment.

As a result, the value of small inexpensive technologies developed locally to meet local needs is now being realised. 2.17 shows an example: an easy-to-use water purification system. It is powered without electricity and is therefore suitable for thousands of Zimbabwean villages where electricity is not available. The Zimbabwean government is encouraging the use of such simple machines to speed up rural development. The machine has only one moving part and two pipe fittings; it is also easy to install and operate. It is made entirely from local materials and simply needs chlorine or other purifying chemicals to be put in the hopper. The machine is placed near a water source or at a central location to which villagers can carry water. It is fairly easy to move and produces 1600 litres of drinking water per hour; enough for more than 80 people a day. One drawback of the machine is its initial cost which, at around £750, is beyond the collective reach of many villages. However, the government may be able to help, or voluntary aid organisations may become involved. Such a machine is also ideal as a small affordable project for which a group of people in the developed world can raise money. Close personal links can be established with the particular village community in the developing world that benefits from the gift.

A Senegal village water supply project

Senegal (2.18), like the other countries of the Sahel (see page 35), suffered long periods of drought in the 1970s and 1980s. Water for village use was traditionally taken from rivers and shallow wells. With rivers low or dried up, the demand for ground water increased and the **water table** (see page 7) fell dangerously low. Water is usually obtained from wells less than 50 metres deep but some have now run completely dry, and water must be obtained from deeper wells. Hauling water up is backbreaking time-consuming work and many women's hands become deformed after years of hauling on the ropes. In the drier north of Senegal, horse and donkey carts are often used to collect water as distances of several kilometres have to be travelled in search of reasonable wells. In the wetter south, distances to wells are shorter and, because of tsetse flies, horses are not generally used, so water is collected on foot and carried by hand.

To improve the water supply to Senegal's villages new bore holes needed to be sunk between 100 and 300 metres down into aquifers (see page 9) where there are safe and reliable supplies of water. Obviously this would mean spending a lot of money, and this was not available in Senegal. A scheme to supply 18 villages with new water supplies was financed by the Overseas Development Administration (ODA) of the British government at a cost of £6 million. Most of the work was carried out by people recruited from the 18 villages; this is very important in gaining a local understanding of how equipment and systems work. As a result of the project, which was carried out from 1983 to 1989, over 85 000 people and 250 000 cattle and sheep have been provided with a safe reliable supply of drinking water.

Planning the project

Before work started on sinking new wells, the two areas of Louga and Casamance (2.19) were surveyed by a study team made up of employees of Balfour Consulting Engineers (employed by the ODA to do the work) and local people. Oxfam was also involved from the planning stage; they helped to organise health education by teaching villagers how to use their new water supplies safely and how to gain the maximum benefit from them. 18 villages were eventually chosen (2.19) and the new water supplies were calculated to meet the demand up to the year 2003 (see table 2.20). During the planning stage the problem of paying for running costs was worked out. Each villager paid about 5p per month on a voluntary basis. This 'tax' was collected by the village council and was used to pay for diesel fuel for the pump and for the salary of the bore hole *gruniad*. The *gruniad* looks after day-to-day maintenance and keeps records of pumping done and fuel used. The villagers do not at the moment pay for all the running costs; the Senegal government meets some. As the benefits build up, it is hoped that the villages will become better off and be able to pay the full running costs, making government funds available to encourage development elsewhere in the country.

Construction

The main features of the project for each village are:
- bore-hole drilling,
- a water tower for storage of about 1 day's supply (2.21a),
- pipes from the tower to distribution points (2.21b) in the village.

Oxfam workers helped to teach the villagers why the new distribution system was necessary. The traditional village well was unhygienic for the following reasons.
- Inadequate drainage around the well head led to stagnant pools of water from spillage, which in time became breeding grounds for mosquitos. These caused disease and illness (see page 8).
- Animals and people used the same well and contamination of drinking water was unavoidable.

The new distribution system for each village has the following advantages.
- Animal watering points have been separated from standpipes by building cattle troughs well outside the village.
- Concrete slabs surround each standpipe (2.21b) and perimeter drains keep watering points dry.
- At least one separate washing area with a large concrete apron and drainage is provided in each village to encourage villagers to keep this operation away from the drinking water collection points.

In addition the bore holes have been sealed to prevent any contamination of the supply.

Measuring success

A number of benefits arose from the scheme apart from the obvious one of a clean water supply for 18 villages.
- Because local people did most of the construction work, a pool of local skilled people was established as the basis for maintenance and day-to-day working.
- By involving the ODA, the Senegalese government, local village people and Oxfam, the project ensured that the whole village community understood and benefited from the project.

The success of the scheme is well demonstrated by the fact that in 1989–90 the villagers of Boudock, Farimboure and Djida Maouda started to build their own extensions to the distribution system. They were directed by their own village management committees who have organised the collection of funds and the purchase of materials.

▼ 2.19

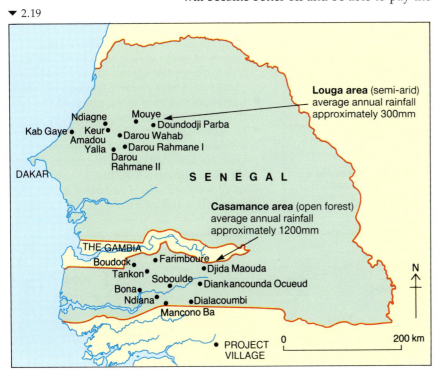

▼ 2.20 Population forecasts

Area	Human population 1983	Human population 2003	Cattle 1983	Cattle 2003	Sheep and goats 1983	Sheep and goats 2003
Louga	56 965	79 855	79 890	118 770	82 610	177 470
Casamance	34 400	49 275	66 845	120 710	40 580	123 955
Total	91 365	129 130	146 735	238 480	123 190	301 425

▼ 2.21a Water tower

▼ 2.21b Water stand

Water 13

Using rivers to the full

In developing countries a major river offers much potential for development: for example, improved water supply, irrigation, power generation and navigation. Sometimes major dams are built at enormous cost and are a clear symbol of development for the rest of the world to see. Money for such dams may be borrowed from organisations such as the World Bank, or come in the form of aid.

The River Nile (2.22) is vital to the development of Egypt, the Sudan and Uganda but there is a limit to its use and many experts agree that this limit is being reached. Also the three user countries are not cooperating fully over the management of the river. The main problems are:

- Annual flow rates of the river have become increasingly variable. Irrigation water is sometimes in short supply and power supplies are threatened by low water levels in the lakes.
- Egypt is abstracting 55.5 billion cubic metres of water a year from the river – 2 billion above the agreed amount – and plans to abstract another 8 billion by 1997.
- Irrigation methods along much of the river are inefficient and wasteful.
- Loss of vegetation cover in Sudan is increasing soil loss and **siltation** rates in Lake Nasser. (Siltation is the rate at which silt builds up on a lake bed.)

What do you think should be done to help overcome these difficulties?

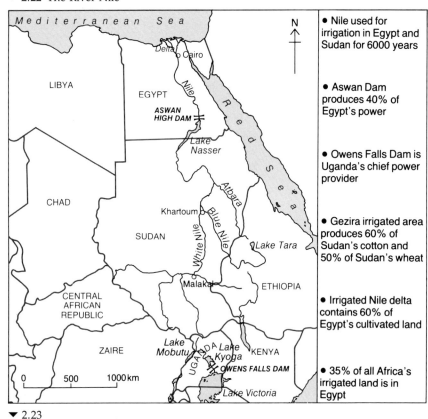

▼ 2.22 The River Nile

- Nile used for irrigation in Egypt and Sudan for 6000 years
- Aswan Dam produces 40% of Egypt's power
- Owens Falls Dam is Uganda's chief power provider
- Gezira irrigated area produces 60% of Sudan's cotton and 50% of Sudan's wheat
- Irrigated Nile delta contains 60% of Egypt's cultivated land
- 35% of all Africa's irrigated land is in Egypt

▼ 2.23

Does India need the Narmada Valley Project?

A start has been made on the biggest water management scheme in history. In the Narmada Valley in western India (2.23) over 3000 dams, large and small, are planned; so huge is the project, that it will take over 100 years to complete. The Indian government thinks the dams will bring great benefits in irrigation and power supplies, but 2.23 suggests why many people are against the scheme. Survival International, a group defending the rights of tribal people (most of the 1 million people affected are tribal people) has been particularly active in trying to persuade the World Bank not to fund the project. What do you think should happen to the scheme?

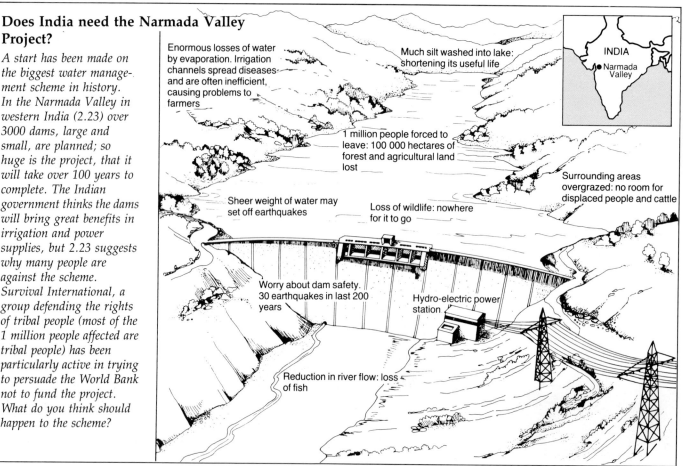

- Enormous losses of water by evaporation. Irrigation channels spread diseases and are often inefficient, causing problems to farmers
- Much silt washed into lake: shortening its useful life
- 1 million people forced to leave: 100 000 hectares of forest and agricultural land lost
- Surrounding areas overgrazed: no room for displaced people and cattle
- Sheer weight of water may set off earthquakes
- Loss of wildlife: nowhere for it to go
- Worry about dam safety. 30 earthquakes in last 200 years
- Hydro-electric power station
- Reduction in river flow: loss of fish

▶ 2.24 Location of Honduras

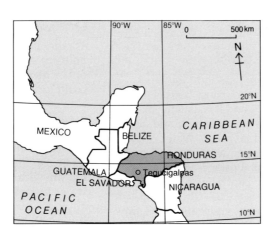

▼ 2.25 The problems facing Tegucigalpas

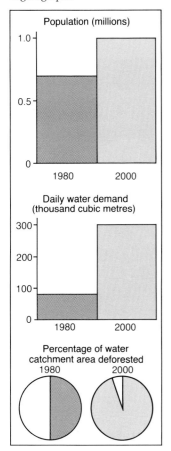

Tegucigalpas: A case study of urban water problems

Tegucigalpas is the capital city of Honduras in Central America (2.24). Many of the inhabitants live in shanty settlements (see page 11) and only two-thirds of the city's people have access to fresh water. Water sellers do a roaring business in the city selling 50-gallon barrels of water at $1.75 each. The water is of poor quality, often collected downstream of points where human and animal waste enters the river. But many people have to buy the water and some families spend half of their income in this way. 2.25 shows some of the problems facing the city. Notice the rapid population growth rate (around 6% per year) and the enormous increase in water demand expected by 2000.

The catchment area from which Tegucigalpas' river water comes used to be forested but, by the year 2000, much of the forest will have been destroyed (2.25), to provide land for shifting agriculture, and wood for fuel. The authorities seem unable to stop the deforestation. For example, the Honduran Corporation of Forestry Development allowed parts of the forest to be destroyed claiming it had no map of the area and was not sure where the boundaries were. Deforestation allows rapid soil erosion and rapid run-off of rain water. With soil and vegetation lost, little water can be temporarily stored and slowly released to rivers via throughflow (see page 7) during dry periods. Ground water supplies (see page 7) are limited and cannot be further developed.

The only way forward seems to be for the Honduran government to try to set up new urban areas. Light industry and businesses must be encouraged to move, taking employees and their families with them. If this cannot be done the water sellers will become richer, but even more people will be denied access to safe drinking water.

Jobs or health?

The Tungabhadra River in the Indian state of Karnataka (2.26) is the lifeblood of the area: animals are watered there, children bathe, crops are irrigated, and people drink (2.27). New factories have sprung up where the local eucalyptus trees are grown as a cash crop to be processed into rayon. Jobs are available in the factories and people are able to earn money; thereby helping the area to develop. But there is an enormous problem. Every day two factories release about 33 000 cubic metres of effluent into the river. Downstream the results of the pollution can be seen. 2.28 describes what was seen by a Christian Aid visitor to the area. The people look ill and grey, and suffer from skin diseases and internal complaints. Some animals have died, and crops irrigated by the chemical-laden water are poor and poisonous. The water is unfit to drink; but there is no other source as the ground water is also contaminated. One factory worker summed up his feelings like this. 'I need the income the factory provides for my family but I hate what the factory is doing to our environment.'

What if anything do you think should be done about the situation?

▼ 2.27

▼ 2.26 Location of Karnataka

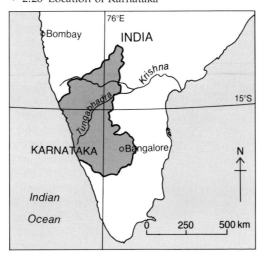

▼ 2.28

We went to look at the landscape around the factory. It was a lovely scene – green banks stretching far into the horizon, blue sky, empty land and a bridge with a little stream train puffing across it. It was beautiful until you realised what was really happening. The little train was bringing more eucalyptus logs to be made into pulp. The land was bare because it was impossible to cultivate. And where the tributary rushed into the river the colour of it made your heart sink. A muddy turbulent gush of water tumbled into the river, a very dark rusty colour, and you could see how thick it was topped with foam, sidling slowly down into the main river of what has been green water before.

(Christian Aid, *Focus on Water Pollution*)

Water 15

Key ideas
- Clean drinking water is readily available in most developed areas.
- Meeting the ever-growing demand for water in developed areas is increasingly costly.

Water
Developed Countries

In developed countries most houses have a piped water supply and it is usually taken for granted that clean safe water is, and always will be, cheap and plentiful. Water can be moved by pipe (**aqueducts**) from areas of surplus to areas of shortage. Drinking water quality is carefully controlled with regular testing and analysis (2.29). Chemical content, acidity, taste, smell and appearance are all monitored. Purifying chemicals are added as necessary to ensure that the water that reaches people's homes is of high quality and poses minimal threats to health.

Demand rises

The demand for water continues to grow, both for use in homes and in industry. One of the major uses of water is for cooling in coal-burning power stations (2.30): around 25% of all the water abstracted in the UK is used in this way (see page 56 for more information on electricity generation).

Because electricity is a convenient, flexible and clean energy source, demand is rising rapidly with a similar rise in the demand for water. People are increasingly able to afford appliances such as dishwashers (2.31) which use much more water than more traditional methods. It is only during times of shortage such as the UK droughts of 1976 and 1989 that we realise just how much we take water for granted.

▲ 2.29 Laboratory testing of water quality

▲ 2.30 Cooling towers

▲ 2.31 Dishwasher

▼ 2.32a Annual water consumption per head in selected countries

▼ 2.32b Uses of water in the USA

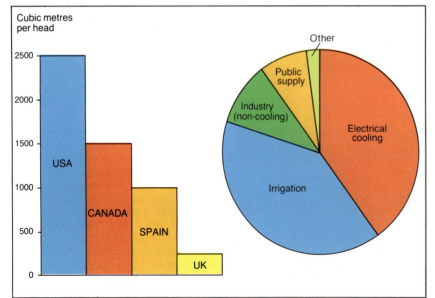

The USA: the thirstiest country in the world

The USA leads the world in water consumption per head of population, the figure being ten times the amount for the UK (2.32a). Notice in 2.32b that water for irrigation and for cooling are the big users. Because the USA is a very rich country it has spent large amounts of money on its water supply systems, but it is becoming increasingly aware that its water supply is limited and is even adopting **water conservation** measures. For example, the Massachusetts Water Authority in the northeast of the country is trying to cut domestic consumption by 40%. However, the demand for irrigation water continues to rise rapidly: the irrigated area increased by 35% between 1970 and 1990 from 150 000 km^2 to well over 200 000 km^2.

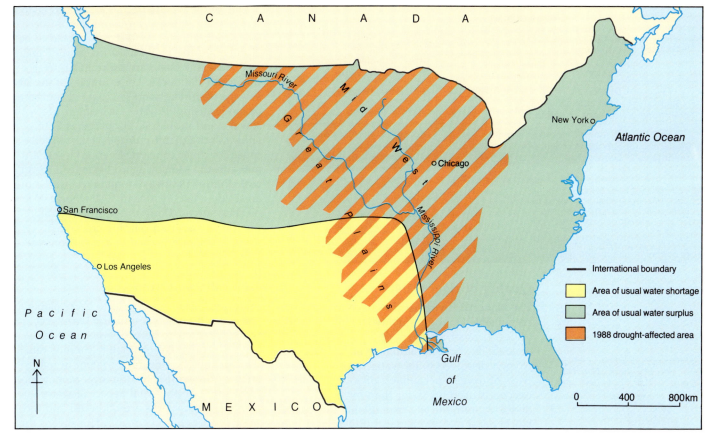

▲ 2.33 Water in the USA

Available water

2.33 shows that most of the northern and eastern states of the USA usually have a **water surplus.** This means that demand can normally be met from the various surface and ground stores. In contrast, much of the south and west is usually short of water (has a **water deficit**). However, periods of drought are a fairly common feature in all central areas (northern as well as southern) and 2.33 shows the extent of the area affected in 1988: water surplus areas became areas of water deficit. Iowa in the mid west (2.33) only received 18 cm of rain in the period January to June compared with the normal 50 cm. Approximately 35% of the country's expected crop yield was lost in 1988 and serious fires broke out in forested areas; 400 000 hectares of woodland in the Yellowstone National Park were destroyed.

Because of the water deficit in the south-western states various stategies have been used to meet the ever-rising demand for water.

- Using more and more ground water.
- Bringing in water by pipe (**aqueducts**) from the north and east.
- Desalinating sea water.

In much of the south-west the population is increasing and the irrigated area is being extended (2.34). Ground water abstraction has nearly tripled since 1950 and water is being taken out faster than it is being replaced (see page 9 for details of aquifers). This means the level of water in the rocks (**water table**) is becoming lower, which allows salt water to enter the aquifers, making the water unfit for use. The problem is so serious in Texas that about 1.5 million hectares of irrigated land may have to be returned to dryland farming by 2020.

Los Angeles (2.33) receives much of its water from wetter areas north of San Francisco via aqueducts. Some people believe the only way to meet the future demands of the area will be to transfer water from as far away as northern Canada. Others see **desalination** of sea water as a possible way to relieve the problems of the rich but water-starved people of Los Angeles. This is a very costly energy-consuming process involving evaporation.

▼ 2.34 Irrigation sprays, Inyo Valley, California

Water 17

Class	Characteristics	Use
1A Unpolluted	Dissolved oxygen high (10 parts per million). Ammonia level very low. No signs of pollution.	Little treatment needed before drinking. Game or other high-class fisheries. High amenity value.
1B Slight pollution	Dissolved oxygen high (9–10 ppm). Ammonia level low. No signs of pollution.	High amenity value.
2 Moderate pollution	Dissolved oxygen 5–9 ppm. Ammonia level moderate. Some pollution can be seen.	Much treatment needed before drinking. Moderate coarse fishing. Moderate amenity value.
3 Severe pollution	Dissolved oxygen low (3–5 ppm). Ammonia level very high. Pollution easily seen.	Industrial abstraction only. Few fish.
4 Gross pollution	Dissolved oxygen very low (< 3 ppm). Ammonia level very high. Pollution easily seen.	River dead, a nuisance and a health hazard.

▲ 2.35 Classification of river water quality

Quality of river water

The National Rivers Authority (NRA) is responsible for water quality in England and Wales. It classifies rivers on a four-point scale (2.35). An unpolluted river has lots of oxygen dissolved in its water (around 10 parts of oxygen per million of water). If this oxygen is used up faster than oxygen dissolves from the air, river quality falls. The biochemical oxygen demand (BOD) is a measure of how much oxygen is being used up by such processes as bacteria feeding on organic matter. Anything with a high BOD is a potential pollutant. Ammonia is a particular destroyer of river quality (2.35) as it has a high BOD and is also poisonous.

2.36 shows the proportions of rivers in each class: notice that about one-third of all rivers are moderately or seriously polluted.

Pollution: threats to quality

There are three main types of pollution which threaten river quality:

- domestic pollution (sewage);
- industrial pollution;
- agricultural pollution.

The NRA monitor pollution levels and prosecute offenders. Some pollution is accidental, some is deliberate, and some is the result of bad planning and a lack of investment. There is increasing public concern about the quality of river water. Many groups such as Friends of the Earth, Greenpeace, and the Green Party bring pressure to bear on the NRA to be tougher with polluters (see Unit 19).

One of the worst affected areas in England is the Mersey Basin. Problems cannot be solved immediately and it is expected to be 2015 before the 1609 km of rivers and canals in the Mersey Basin are brought up to minimum standards. For example, of the 200 sewage treatment works, 150 need replacing or modernising. Progress is being made with sewage and industrial discharge as 2.37 shows, but agricultural pollution is still a cause for great concern. Even if targets are met and the Mersey again becomes a clean river there will always remain the threat of an accident like the one in 1989 when a 40 km oil slick spread along the northern bank of the Mersey after an oil pipe cracked.
What do you think should be done to minimise the effects of accidents like this?

Domestic pollution

We expect clean safe water to be available to use in our homes and similarly we expect our waste products to be properly treated in sewage works. Unfortunately there is much wrong with the sewerage system in many areas of the world. Not enough money has been spent on this vital aspect of water management. Works are often old and too small for present-day needs. This means that not all sewage is properly treated before being returned to rivers or the sea. A particular problem exists in many coastal towns where raw (untreated) sewage is pumped directly into the sea at low tide.

Major problems occur when sewage and rain water mix after heavy rainfall. Sewage works cannot cope with this extra volume and the overspill means that the contents of a city's lavatories are discharged straight into a river. When sewage enters a river, bacteria in the water increase rapidly as they break down the sewage and this causes the BOD to shoot up. The oxygen level in the water may fall so low that bacteria are unable to live and then the river becomes an open sewer supporting no life.

The main task of a sewage works (2.38) is to speed up the natural breakdown of

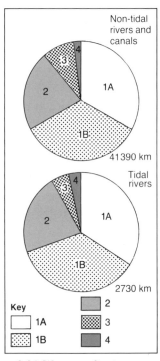

▲ 2.36 Water quality in England and Wales

▼ 2.37 Water quality changes, Mersey Basin, 1983–6

Pollution source	Improvement (km)	Deterioration (km)	Change
Sewers	27	10	+17
Industrial discharges	18	6	+12
Agricultural chemicals	1	43	−42
Others	19	64	−48
Total	65	123	−58

▼ 2.38 Sewage works

18 Water

sewage by bacteria. To compensate for the increased BOD, the oxygen level of the sewage is increased artificially (**aeration**). After purification, water of an acceptable quality can be returned to the river and the solid waste remaining may be used as a fertiliser (if it does not contain dangerous chemicals) or dumped on land or in the sea.

▼ 2.39 Pollution on the River Rhine

- 30 tonnes of agricultural chemicals entered the Rhine in Basle in 1986
- 20 million people use the Rhine for drinking water: alternative supplies needed while pollution surge passed
- Pollution in three countries
- A long stretch of the river will remain ecologically dead for 10 years

Industrial pollution

Industrial processes such as chemical manufacture and electroplating pose serious potential threats to rivers. Cyanide or solutions of heavy metals such as copper and zinc can be discharged into rivers as industrial waste. Spillages, even quite small ones, are another serious problem: 4 litres of carbolic acid needs to be diluted 1000 million times before it is safe. Spillages of beer and milk into rivers are especially dangerous as these products have a very high BOD.

2.39 gives details of a spillage incident at a manufacturing plant in Basle, Switzerland, in 1986 where in 2 hours more agricultural chemicals were washed into the river than it normally receives during a whole year. The chemicals killed the daphnia (water fleas) which form the basis of the Rhine food chains, as well as eels which are regarded as a hardy species. The effects of this accident are likely to be felt well after 1995 and there is still great concern that the chemicals will contaminate ground water by percolation through the river bed.

Agricultural pollution

Agricultural activity causes river pollution through three main sources of contamination:

- excess fertiliser, especially nitrates, washed off the soil;
- solid and liquid manure, and silage effluent (waste water from a grass silage clamp);
- pesticides washed into water courses.

In the last 30 years the quantity of nitrogen-based fertiliser used in agriculture has increased 500% in the UK. It is usually added to the soil by spreading in granule form (2.40). Nitrates are easily taken in by plant roots but equally readily dissolve in the rain water that moves through the soil by throughflow (see page 7) and enters water courses. Ideally farmers should spread much smaller amounts at regular intervals but this is expensive. Excess nitrates in drinking water are a danger to our health. In rivers and lakes they cause **eutrophication**: the excess of nutrients causes abundant growth of plants and animals. These algal blooms can be very dangerous to wildlife and humans. Denmark has taken the lead in reducing fertiliser consumption (2.41) as part of a 'Water Environment Plan' due to be fully in force by 1994.

Intensive animal production produces two highly dangerous products. Slurry (liquid manure) is 100 times, and silage effluent 200 times, more polluting than untreated domestic sewage. In spite of laws and prosecution by the NRA, these twin problems are getting worse. Proper safe slurry storage is essential so that spreading can be restricted to the growing season when the nutrients are taken up by plants. A **biogas digester** can be used to convert slurry into gas which can be used as a fuel. 40 tonnes of slurry per day will give enough energy to heat a village of 130 homes and the degassed residue makes a 'safe' fertiliser.

The European Community sets 'safe' limits on pesticide concentration in water but there is much dispute about these and many people think some pesticides should be banned altogether.

What are your views on the use of pesticides? How do you think the views of a farmer might differ?

▲ 2.40 Nitrogen spreading

▼ 2.41 Use of nitrogen fertiliser in Denmark

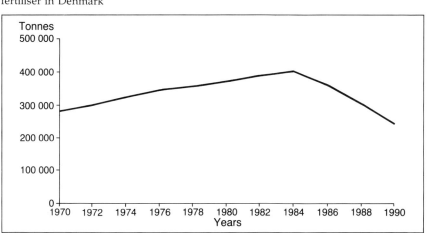

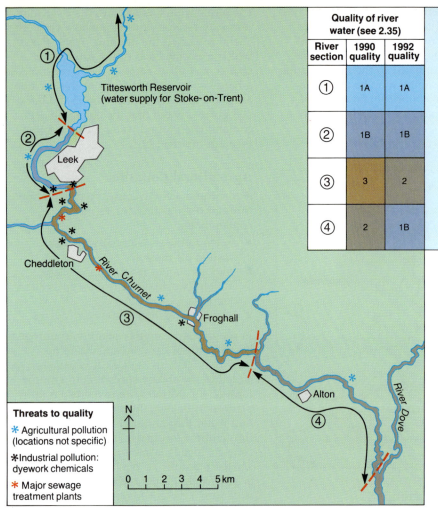

▲ 2.42 Pollution on the River Churnet

The Churnet: a heavily polluted river

The River Churnet rises north of Leek in Staffordshire (2.42) and flows 43 km before joining the River Dove. Its good-quality soft water (containing very few chemicals from rocks) originally attracted a number of industries, particularly the dyeing industry. However, the river is now seriously polluted for a number of reasons. The Severn Trent Water Authority is tackling the problem and attempting to improve the water quality.

Look at the two newspaper articles below.

(a) *Describe and explain the problem.*
(b) *Discuss what is being done to tackle it.*
(c) *Explain why problems like this take a long time to rectify.*

▶ 2.43 *Leek Post and Times*, 2 March 1988

CHURNET 'MOST POLLUTED' SHOCK

THE RIVER Churnet is now so polluted that the Severn Trent Water Authority is unable to meet its own minimum required standards.

The 50-year-old Cheddleton treatment works can no longer cope with the amount of waste being pumped into public sewers. Therefore, says the water authority, it is forced to discharge unsatisfactorily treated effluent into the river.

Severn Trent is particularly concerned at the big rise in the volume of trade waste being discharged illegally.

'We cannot cope with what the traders are throwing at us,' explained Severn Trent's area quality officer, Mr Tony Stanley. 'That means that we are discharging effluent below our own standards.'

The Churnet, which flows through some of the most picturesque countryside in North Staffordshire, is now the most polluted river in the area. Severn Trent has a rating system from one to four for all its waterways with class one being the highest quality. The Churnet is rated as class three, very poor, according to Mr Stanley.

'At the moment we are trying to get it up to class two,' he said. 'It is one of my highest priorities to get the river cleaned up.'

The situation has become more acute over the last few years because of the massive increase in the volume of industrial waste, much of which is being discharged illegally.

Severn Trent has already demonstrated that it intends to prosecute firms who break the regulations and Mr Stanley warned that more cases against such companies would follow.

▼ 2.44 *Stoke Evening Sentinel*, 17 September 1988

RIVER SET FOR CLEAN-UP

SEVERN TRENT officials have unveiled a £9 million scheme to combat water pollution from industrial waste in the River Churnet.

The water authority says if cash is not spent now on tackling pollution Staffordshire will be out of line when stricter Government controls come into force.

Improvements to the sewage treatment works at Leek and Cheddleton will cost £9 million.

A total of £8 million will be spent at the Leek plant where dye dumped in the water by local clothing manufacturers is a major cause of pollution.

STWA district manager Mr Craig Reid said the £8 million scheme would increase Leek's capacity to deal with sewage, as well as help purify water polluted by clothing dye.

Anglers will also benefit from the improved sewage control, which Mr Reid believes will help attract more fish back into the River Churnet.

'At present the river does not support as big a fish population as it should. But it is hoped the improvements at Leek will produce good quality coarse fishing,' he said.

The £1 million earmarked for the Cheddleton works will go towards further improvements in the sewage treatment process at the plant.

It is estimated work at Cheddleton will be completed by 1990 and at Leek by 1991.

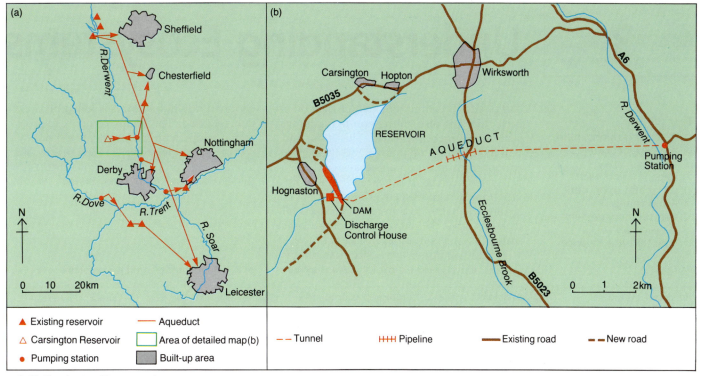

▲ 2.45 Carsington Dam supply area

▼ 2.46a East Midlands summer season: demands and resources

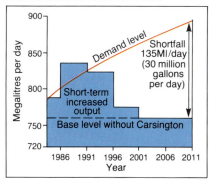

▼ 2.46b Carsington Dam under construction

▼ 2.46c Artist's impression of finished dam and reservoir

Future water for the East Midlands

Over 3 million people in the East Midlands (Derbyshire, Nottinghamshire and Leicestershire) get much of their water from the upper Trent drainage basin (2.45a). A new reservoir is being built at Carsington to take water from the Derwent during winter and times of plenty, and return it to the river during times of need for additional public water supplies. Notice that the reservoir is connected to the Derwent by an aqueduct which is largely underground (2.45b).

The reason for Carsington being built can be seen on 2.46a. The reservoir will be able to supply over 200 megalitres a day which will more than meet the demand until well beyond 2011. Without the reservoir there could be major water shortages by the year 2000.

Work on the scheme started in 1980 but stopped abruptly in 1984 when part of the dam collapsed (2.46b). The collapse caused much concern especially in villages such as Hognaston downstream of the dam. It took five years to sort out what went wrong and to agree on the changes needed to make the dam safe. As well as providing water for the 'distant' towns of the East Midlands the reservoir will

- provide local recreational amenities such as angling and sailing;
- bring the benefits of by-pass roads to three local villages (2.45b).

Draw up a table to compare the positive and negative effects of the dam from the point of view of the local population.

Water 21

3 Understanding Ecosystems

Key ideas
- The living things in an area are delicately balanced; they depend upon each other and upon non-living things.
- Careful management is necessary to maintain this balance.

The plants and animals of an area depend on each other and also on the non-living things, such as air, rock and water. The living and non-living things of an area and their inter-relationships make up an **ecosystem**. Ecosystems can be of any size ranging from a vast tropical rainforest covering thousands of square kilometres to a small pond just a few metres square. 3.1 shows some of the large-scale ecosystems in different areas of the world. Living things are easily changed by human activity; for example, trees may be chopped down and animals killed or domesticated. The highly complex inter-relationships within ecosystems are not completely understood, so human interference can be an enormous threat to the existence of many ecosystems.

▼ 3.1 Some of the world's ecosystems

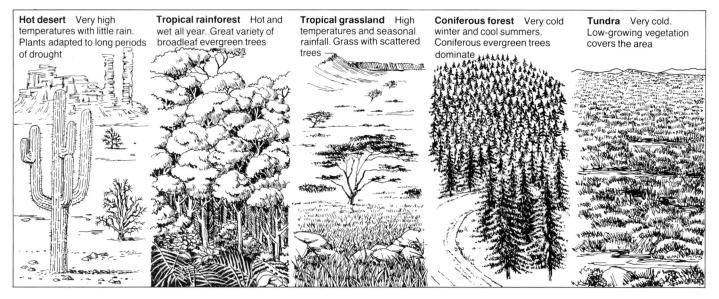

Hot desert Very high temperatures with little rain. Plants adapted to long periods of drought

Tropical rainforest Hot and wet all year. Great variety of broadleaf evergreen trees

Tropical grassland High temperatures and seasonal rainfall. Grass with scattered trees

Coniferous forest Very cold winter and cool summers. Coniferous evergreen trees dominate

Tundra Very cold. Low-growing vegetation covers the area

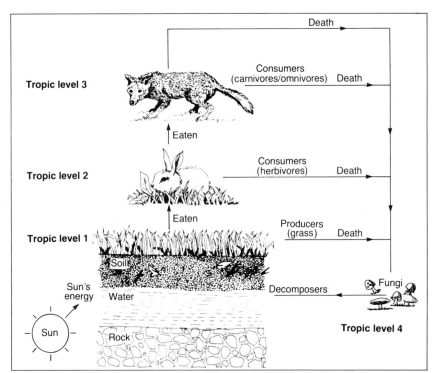

◀ 3.2 System diagram of an ecosystem

3.2 gives information about how all ecosystems are organised, using the example of a grass field in the UK. Notice that the energy for driving the system comes from the sun and that the system is divided into a number of **compartments** called **trophic levels**. The grasses in trophic level 1 provide the foundation for the whole system and are called **producers**. The energy from the sun is taken in by plants and used to make them grow, producing leaves, roots, etc. The producer plants are **consumed** by animals, so the energy is transferred along a chain called a **food chain**. Death is also vital to the ecosystem, as when plants and animals die they are broken down or decomposed by fungi and bacteria in the soil. Minerals are released and can be used again as they are reabsorbed through the roots of the next generation of producers. Table 3.4 explains more about some of the terms used in describing the workings of ecosystems.

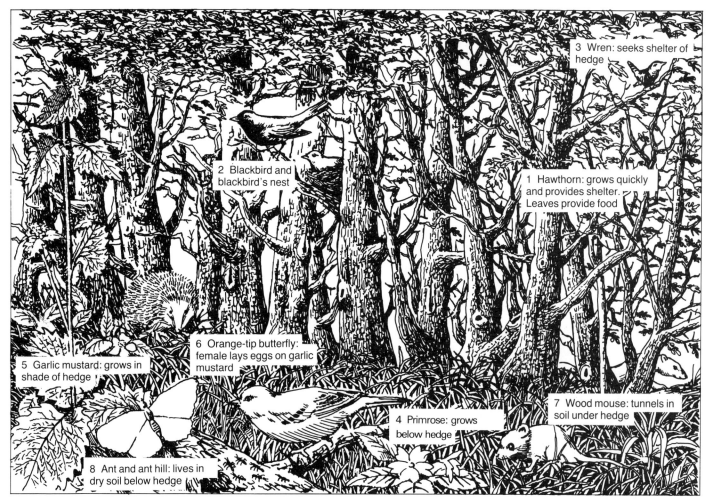

▲ 3.3 The hedgerow ecosystem: Britain's biggest nature reserve

▼ 3.4 Important ecosystem terms

Producers. Plants in trophic level 1 of an ecosystem. This level is also called the **primary production** of the ecosystem.

Biomass. The weight of vegetation in a fixed area of an ecosystem. Usually expressed as dry kilograms per square metre.

Consumers. Animals which eat vegetation (**herbivores**) or eat other animals (**carnivores**). **Omnivores** eat both plants and animals.

Decomposers. Bacteria and fungi which break down dead producers and consumers and so allow the recycling of nutrients.

Food chain. The transfer of energy through an ecosystem from producers to consumers. In reality the transfer is very complex with many food chains inter-related to form a **food web**.

The Hedgerow Ecosystem

3.3 gives information about the hedgerow ecosystem in Britain. Unlike the examples in 3.1, the hedgerow is not a natural ecosystem because the hedges were planted to divide up land into fields and to provide shelter. The natural ecosystems in 3.1 are the result of gradual change over a very long period of time, often thousands of years. In Britain the oak forest was probably the most common natural ecosystem. Some 7000–10 000 years ago much of Britain was covered with glacial debris after the Ice Age and there was little proper soil. Simple plants like lichens grew first and, as the soil improved, more advanced plants with deeper roots took over. This process is called **plant succession** and the most advanced plants at the end of the succession are the **climate climax vegetation**.

Notice on 3.3 how the producer plants and the consumer animals all fit logically together. For example, the garlic mustard is a shade-loving plant and so finds the area beneath the hedge an ideal place to grow. Each plant or animal has an **ecological niche** in the hedgerow where conditions suit its particular needs. There are many ecological niches in the hedgerow, making it a very rich ecosystem for plants and wildlife.

Look carefully at 3.3 and see how many ecological niches you can identify.

Upsetting the system

Because so much of lowland Britain is used for agriculture the hedgerow has become an important nature reserve. Many people are concerned about threats to hedgerows which will reduce the variety of wildlife found in the British countryside. The main threats are as follows.

- The complete removal of hedgerows to make fields larger and to allow machinery to operate more efficiently. (Their removal also allows more land to be cultivated and therefore increases crop production.)
- The use of pesticides on fields, which can drift into hedgerows and cause damage. Even if all the pesticide remains on the crop, birds and animals will feed on the crop and so allow the chemicals to enter the food webs of the hedgerow.

Bearing in mind that Britain has a surplus of many sorts of crops, suggest what could be done to maintain and increase the hedgerows in the countryside.

Understanding Ecosystems

4 Soil

Key idea
- Soil is a complex substance and needs careful management to prevent it being damaged by human activity.

Soil Contents

4.1 gives information about the make-up of soil. A fertile soil needs a good balance of the different components. The grains of rock (e.g. sand and clay) and some of the minerals come from the **parent material** of the area. This is usually a solid rock (e.g. sandstone) or a covering of broken rock particles of varying sizes (e.g. material left behind after glaciation). As the parent material is weathered (broken down into smaller pieces, without being moved away) by such things as frost and rain, a basic 'soil' forms. Plants start to grow and in time they die and rot with the help of **decomposers** (see page 23) to form **humus**. The humus contains minerals which enrich the soil, and the humus also helps the soil to hold water.

A fully developed soil takes a long time to form (at least several hundreds of years). The formation of topsoil and subsoil layers (photo 4.1) indicate a fully developed soil.

▼ 4.1 Soil contents

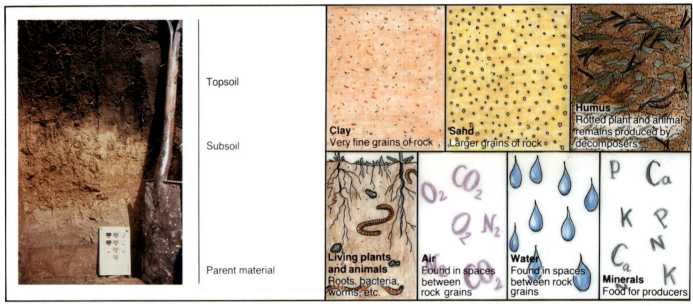

▼ 4.2 Two types of soil: tropical red and UK brown earth

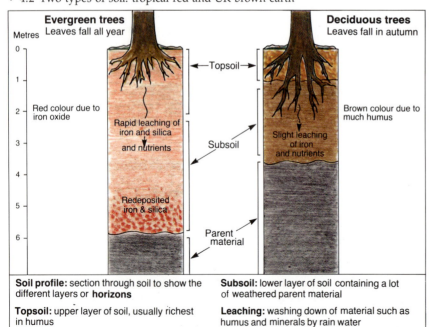

Soil profile: section through soil to show the different layers or **horizons**

Topsoil: upper layer of soil, usually richest in humus

Subsoil: lower layer of soil containing a lot of weathered parent material

Leaching: washing down of material such as humus and minerals by rain water

Soil Processes

Different soils *look* very different and their **soil profiles** differ in depth and make-up (4.2). These differences are due to the many processes at work in forming soil. The main ones are as follows.

- The weathering of the parent material to provide some of the basic soil components.
- The vegetation type which provides the humus.
- The climate which influences weathering and vegetation and also the movement of water within soil. **Leaching** (4.2) is a very important process which affects many soils.
- The slope of the land on which the soil forms. Soil is thin and poorly developed on steep slopes, and deep and well developed on flatter areas.

Human activity constantly threatens the fertility of soil, especially when vegetation is cleared or modified. Despite a much greater understanding of the processes at work in soil and ecosystems, much damage is still being done to soil in both developed and developing areas of the world.

▼ 4.3 Main causes of soil erosion

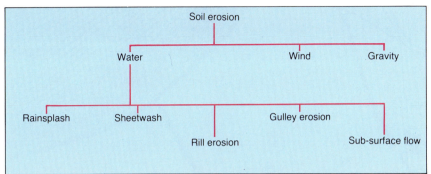

Upsetting the Balance

The UK **brown earth** soil (4.2) is a fertile soil for farmers but, as soon as the deciduous trees are felled to grow crops, the balance of the entire ecosystem is upset. Farmers try to rectify this by such things as

- adding animal manure, plant humus and artificial fertilisers to make up for the humus and minerals no longer being supplied by leaves;
- ploughing the soil to keep the soil correctly aerated and drained to compensate for the loss of tree roots and a greater soil animal life which used to do this;
- including a period of **fallow** every few years to allow the land to rest and recover some of its former fertility.

Despite these measures things sometimes go seriously wrong and **soil erosion** (loss of soil) occurs. Some soil erosion occurs in Britain (pages 26, 27) but the problems are much greater in developing areas which are often desperately trying to increase food output to feed a rapidly growing population.

4.3 shows the main causes of soil erosion. Erosion by water and gravity occurs on slopes, whereas wind erosion occurs on both slopes and flat land.

Wind erosion is often triggered by **overgrazing** in areas of low rainfall. Too many animals are kept, the grass leaves are grazed to the ground and in time the roots die, leaving bare soil which is easily blown away. Ploughing in semi-arid areas can have a similar effect because the protective vegetation cover is lost.

Problems and Solutions in Central America

In Central America the effects of soil erosion by water and gravity are considerable. The soil is mainly a deep tropical red soil (see 4.2) which is formed under evergreen rainforest. When the forest is cleared, problems are severe.

4.4a shows **sheet erosion** (or sheetwash) where the force of water flowing (like a sheet) down a slope carries fertile topsoil away with it. Notice how the upper slope is not affected.

4.4b shows erosion in **rills** and small gulleys where topsoil is removed by a line of water flowing down a slope. The problem has been made worse by planting the crops up and down the slope.

4.4c shows topsoil and subsoil being eroded where several gulleys come together.

Rainsplash takes place on all slopes where bare soil is exposed. As a drop of rain hits the soil, the particles of soil splatter upwards in all directions. When the particles fall back due to gravity more of them land on the downslope sides of the original point of impact than on the upslope. This happens many millions of times during rainfall, resulting in the gradual movement of soil down the slope.

4.4d shows the re-establishment of a vegetation cover to control erosion, and 4.4e shows the planting of crops along the contours, and the construction of terraces to control run-off water.

▼ 4.4a Sheetwash

▼ 4.4b Rills and gulleys

▼ 4.4c Topsoil and subsoil

▼ 4.4d Re-establishment of vegetation cover

▼ 4.4e Contour planting and terracing

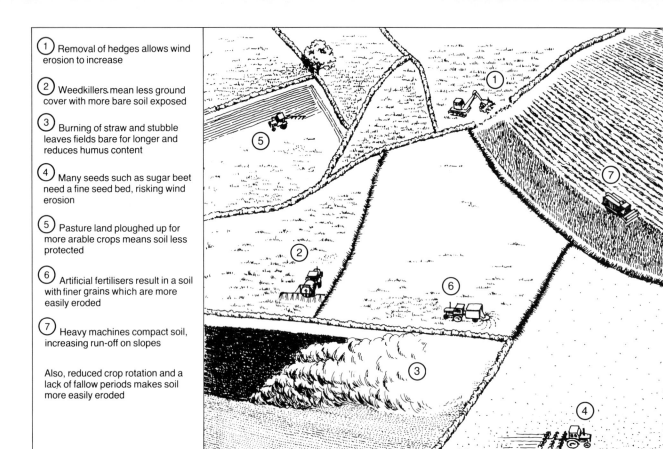

1. Removal of hedges allows wind erosion to increase
2. Weedkillers mean less ground cover with more bare soil exposed
3. Burning of straw and stubble leaves fields bare for longer and reduces humus content
4. Many seeds such as sugar beet need a fine seed bed, risking wind erosion
5. Pasture land ploughed up for more arable crops means soil less protected
6. Artificial fertilisers result in a soil with finer grains which are more easily eroded
7. Heavy machines compact soil, increasing run-off on slopes

Also, reduced crop rotation and a lack of fallow periods makes soil more easily eroded

▲ 4.5 Causes of soil erosion

Soil Erosion in Britain

Erosion of agricultural soil by wind and water is a growing problem in many parts of Britain. Modern agricultural practices, especially in the arable areas of eastern England, are largely responsible. 4.5 shows some of the causes. The agricultural industry has constantly increased productivity for many years but there is now growing evidence that soil quality is suffering and that action must be taken. Wind erosion (4.6) is a particular problem in areas of light humus-rich soil. The danger is greatest in spring when the bare soil is exposed, before the newly planted crops can provide a protective cover. Severe wind erosion can take place in a matter of hours and, after bad 'blows', whole fields may have to be reseeded.

Water erosion is a more widespread problem but generally less spectacular. Rills several centimetres deep are often formed on sloping arable fields with seeds either being washed out on upper slopes or buried by deposited soil on lower slopes. Surprisingly large amounts of soil can be lost: annual rates of removal of over 240 tonnes per hectare have been recorded, equivalent to surface lowering of 12 millimetres.

There are many ways in which the situation can be improved (4.7). But many farmers still do not recognise the problem as serious, partly because most British soils are quite resilient and can withstand quite a lot of bad management before major problems arise.

▼ 4.6 Wind erosion

▼ 4.7 Managing soil erosion

Action taken	Control over		
	Rainsplash	Run-off	Wind
Cover soil e.g. plant trees or grass	Much improvement	Much improvement	Much improvement
Increase surface roughness e.g. no fine harrowing	No effect	Much improvement	Much improvement
Increase surface storage	Some improvement	Much improvement	No effect
Increase infiltration e.g. 'spike' soil	No effect	Much improvement	No effect
Use fertilisers and manure	No effect	No effect	Much improvement
Improve drainage	No effect	Much improvement	No effect
Contour ploughing	No effect	Much improvement	Some improvement
Terracing	No effect	Much improvement	No effect
Plant shelter belts	No effect	No effect	Much improvement

Key: No effect / Some improvement / Much improvement

4.8a shows how a large 61 hectare field in North Norfolk was originally formed from 10 small fields. However, erosion became a major problem and crop yields of wheat and sugar beet were falling. 4.8b shows a proposed new plan for dividing up the field. *Use the information on the maps and on page 26 to describe and explain the types of erosion likely to occur in plan (a) and suggest how the problems can be tackled in the new arrangement (b).*

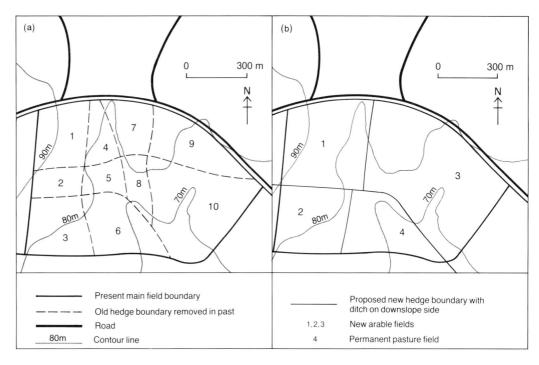

▶ 4.8 Changes in a Norfolk field

Look carefully at 4.9 and, for each section of the record sheet, try to explain why the Soil Association require the information.

▶ 4.9 Soil Watch record sheet

Some people believe that **organic farming** techniques should be more widely used. Organic farming is a 'soil-enhancing' system which, unlike intensive conventional farming, does not use chemical fertilisers or pesticides. It involves minimum soil erosion, and helps to solve other environmental problems such as nitrate fertiliser being washed off the soil into water sources (see page 19), and pesticide damage.

Britain has a surplus of many arable crops, and a 'set-aside scheme', in which farmers are paid to leave their land fallow, has also been suggested to help conserve soil. However this approach could be dangerous because it may not reduce the intensive pressure on the land remaining in production, and may even increase the pressure and so increase the rate of erosion.

Soil Watch

As we become more aware of the damage that intensive and specialised agriculture is doing to soil, there is a need to have much more information about the occurrence of soil erosion. 4.9 is a record sheet produced by the Soil Association (an organisation concerned with the study and effective management of soil by organic farming methods). The idea is to help individuals who are interested in and concerned about the countryside to recognise the signs of erosion, even in its early stages. The sheet outlines some basic checks that can easily be carried out at the sites of erosion. The information is then passed on to scientists studying soil erosion. By making use of ordinary visitors to the countryside, the record-sheet system is designed to increase significantly the proportion of the country surveyed for erosion, and to locate trouble spots not previously identified. The Soil Association recommend that the checks are done from March to May when soil is often bare. If erosion has been bad enough to carry away or bury part of the crop this will remain evident for some time after the crops have covered the less affected parts of the field.

5 Forest Ecosystems

Key ideas
- Forests of various sorts cover large areas of the earth's surface.
- There is increasing concern about the loss of forest ecosystems.

About one-third of the land surface of the earth is covered by forest. 5.1 shows the distribution of the main forest types. On a world scale, climate is the major influence on forest type.

- Tropical rainforests have high temperatures (25–30 °C) all year round and plenty of rain (1500 mm per year).
- Broadleaf forests have a seasonal range of temperature (0–25 °C) and about 600 mm of rain per year.
- Coniferous forests have cold winters (−10 °C) and cool summers (15 °C) with low rainfall (less than 400 mm per year).

More information about rainforests and coniferous forests is shown in 5.3 and 5.4 on page 29.

Forest ecosystems are the most **productive** of the natural ecosystems (5.2). They all have a large amount of living plant material or **biomass** (see page 23). The tropical rainforest alone accounts for nearly 50% of the world biomass. On average three-quarters of the biomass in a mature forest is in the trees. The remaining quarter is in other plants which grow on the trees or in the soil beneath the trees. The biomass production also varies within the different climatic ecosystems (5.2). This is due to such things as:

- the quality of the soil, especially water and nutrient content;
- the age of the forest;
- the impact of people.

Look at 5.1 and describe the amounts and types of forest found in the different world areas.
Look at 5.2. Compare the figures and attempt to explain why they differ.

▼ 5.2 Ecosystems in production

Ecosystem	Area (millions km²)	Plant production per unit area (dry g/m²/yr)		Biomass per unit area (dry kg/m²)		World biomass (billions dry tonnes)
		Range	Average	Range	Average	
Tropical rainforest	20	1000–5000	2000	6–80	45	900
Broadleaf forest	18	600–2500	1300	6–200	30	540
Coniferous forest	12	400–2000	800	6–40	20	240
Savanna (tropical) grassland	15	200–2000	700	0.2–15	4	60
Agricultural land	14	100–4000	650	0.4–12	1	14
Total land	149		730		12.5	1852

▼ 5.1 Distribution of main forest types

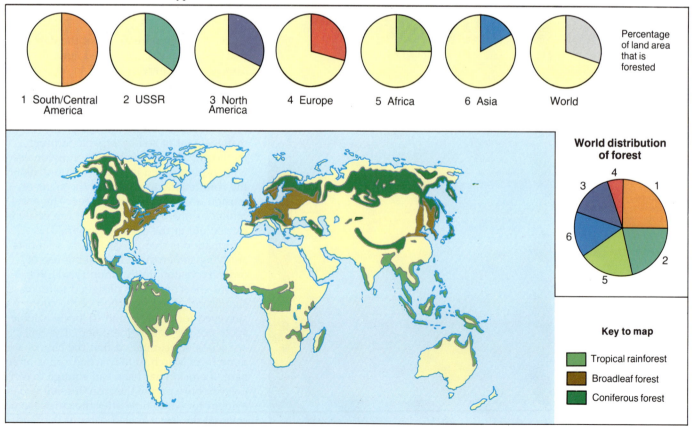

28 Forest Ecosystems

Tropical Rainforest

Main features:

- hardwood trees such as mahogany and teak;
- many different species of tree in a small area (**mixed stands**);
- large evergreen leaves allow rapid growth all year in ideal climate;
- most nutrients are released by decomposers near the soil surface so roots are shallow and buttress roots help to support the tree;
- the ecosystem can be easily disrupted – if trees are destroyed, this results in loss of humus and nutrients, and also exposes the soil to erosion by heavy rain.

Most tropical rainforest is found in developing countries, but the area of forest is being reduced at an alarming rate. This is causing great concern in both the developing and the developed worlds.

Coniferous Forest

Main features:

- softwood trees such as pine and spruce;
- often a single species dominates a large area (**pure stands**);
- needle-shaped evergreen leaves allow growth in summer and, because of their small surface area, allow winter survival;
- nutrients released very slowly near the surface so roots are shallow; trees not as tall as emergents in rainforest so buttress roots are not needed;
- the ecosystem is quite resilient as humus remains in the soil; erosion by rain can be a problem.

Most coniferous forest is found in developed countries. The forest area remains fairly constant because of effective management of the resource.

▼ 5.3 Tropical rainforest cross-section

▼ 5.4 Coniferous forest cross-section

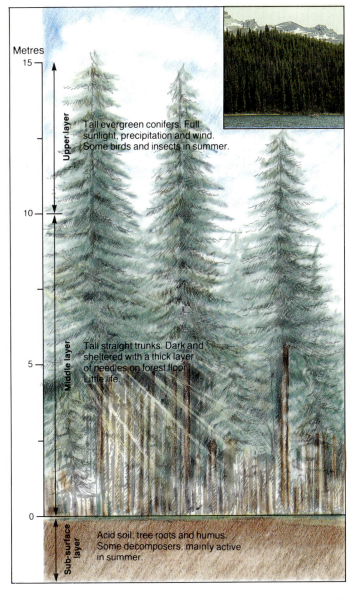

Forest Ecosystems

▲ 5.5 South American Indians

▲ 5.6 Rainforest destruction

GOING,...
Ivory Coast. Forest almost logged out.
Congo. 68% of rainforest scheduled to be logged.
Indonesia. 200 000 hectares logged a year. 10% of its 1981 forest will be destroyed by 2000.
Thailand. 60% of its 1981 forest will be lost by 2000.
Nigeria. Complete deforestation expected by 2000.
Guinea. 33% of its forest will be lost by 2000.
Madagascar will lose 30% of its forest by 2000.

GOING,...
Ghana will lose 25% of remaining forest by 2000.
Nicaragua will lose over 50% of remaining forest by 2000.
Ecuador will lose over 50% of remaining forest by 2000.
Colombia will lose 33% of remaining forest by 2000.
Brazil. Contains about one-third of the world's 900 million hectares of rainforest in the Amazon region. 63 million hectares will be lost by 2000: an area 2.5 times bigger than Portugal.

GONE
Philippines. 55% of forest lost between 1960 and 1985.
Thailand. 45% of forest lost between 1961 and 1985.
India. All original rainforest destroyed.
Bangladesh. All original rainforest destroyed.
Sri Lanka. Almost all original rainforest destroyed.
Haiti. All original rainforest destroyed.
China. 50% of forest lost in Xishuangbana Province.
WORLD. Over 40% of tropical rainforests destroyed.

▲ 5.7

▼ 5.8 Some effects of removing the rainforest

- **Soil erosion.** Without the canopy protection and root binding, soil is easily washed away by the heavy rainfall.
- **Soil infertility.** Even if it is not washed away, the soil rapidly becomes infertile because of leaching of nutrients and a lack of humus from leaf fall.
- **Increased flooding.** Without the forest cover, rapid run-off of rain results, causing serious river flooding.
- **Global warming.** Without the large areas of forests to absorb carbon dioxide from the air, the world may become warmer and drier. The extra carbon dioxide in the air contributes to the 'greenhouse effect', keeping more of the earth's heat in. Burning forest also produces extra carbon dioxide.
- **Loss of plant and animal life.** A valuable store of resources is lost (see 5.9 for some uses of plants as medicines).

Rainforest Destruction

Native people in tropical regions have lived in harmony with rainforests for thousands of years (5.5), but today between 11 and 15 million hectares of forest are damaged or destroyed each year (5.6). Unless things change, there will be no undamaged rainforest left by 2070. The main reasons for forest destruction are:

- to make money from selling timber to developed countries;
- to make money from selling cash crops or cattle produced on cleared land to developed countries (particularly those such as the USA with a high demand for beef);
- to allow local people to grow more food;
- to provide firewood for local people.

5.7 shows how widespread and serious the forest loss is.

Rainforest loss is very serious because the forest is a valuable **resource** for the **whole world**, not just for the particular countries in which the forest grows. 5.8 shows some of the general effects of forest loss, and 5.9 gives details of some of the uses for medicines obtained from rainforest plants. Only about 1% of tropical rainforest species have been examined for their use in life-saving drugs, and clearly the possibilities for the future are immense. Much knowledge about the use of forest products in medicine has already been discovered by traditional tribes, but this and other knowledge is threatened by the loss of these tribes.

Most rainforest destruction is a desperate attempt to ease problems of poverty in developing countries, but developed countries also contribute by continuing to buy hardwood timber and beef. On the next page are examples of positive steps being taken to tackle the problems of rainforest loss. Unit 19 (pages 90–3) suggests how individuals in a developed country like Britain can also play a part.

▼ 5.9 Uses of rainforest plants as medicines

Malaria: treated with *quinine* from the cinchona tree of Peru.

Surgery: great use made of *d-turbocurarine*, a muscle relaxant made from *curare* which comes from a liana in Brazil.

Amoebic dysentery: treated with *ipecac*, a plant from South American rainforests.

Birth control: a major ingredient of the contraceptive pill is *diosgenin* from wild yams of Mexico and Guatemala.

Hypertension: treated with *resperine* from a shrub of South East Asian forests.

Barbiturate overdose: breathing is restored with *picrotoxin*, a berry of South East Asian forests.

Glaucoma: treated with *diosgenin* from West African calabar bean.

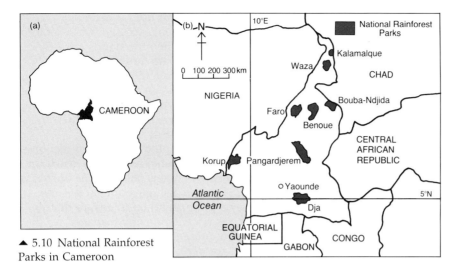

▲ 5.10 National Rainforest Parks in Cameroon

▼ 5.11 Agro-forestry

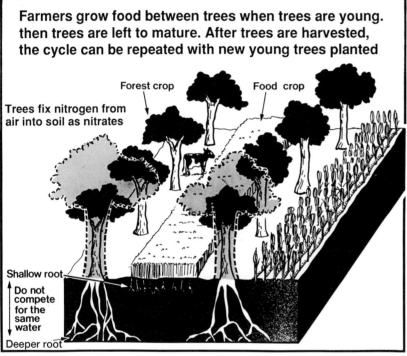

▼ 5.12 *The Independent*, 23 December 1987

Rainforest Protection

Cameroon National Rainforest Parks

Over half of the rainforests in Africa have been cleared. Some of the most extensive areas remaining are in the United Republic of Cameroon (5.10a). The Cameroon government realises that the successful management and development of forests is essential for economic progress. A network of National Rainforest Parks (NRPs) is to be established (5.10b) covering 11 000 km^2 and representing 10% of the world's protected forest. A survey of Korup NRP (see 5.10b) found 17 tree species and 38 substances of possible economic value which were previously unknown.

The cost of establishing and managing the parks is being met by:

- the Cameroon government;
- international support from organisations such as Earthlife and the World Wide Fund for Nature.

Agro-forestry: the best of both worlds

The idea behind agro-forestry is to combine farming and forestry to reduce forest losses and prevent soil erosion. One idea is to grow cash crops under trees which improve soil fertility by 'fixing' nitrogen from the air into the soil (5.11). The idea is only experimental but research is planned to go on until at least 2001. The research is being carried out in Kenya, by the Canadian International Development Research Centre. As in the Cameroon programme, developing and developed countries are working together to tackle the problems of rainforest loss. To date agro-forestry experiments have been very successful, and the system seems well suited to the small farming units in most developing countries.

VANISHING tropical rainforests along Brazil's Atlantic seaboard, which are home to two of the world's rarest monkeys, have been given the highest priority in the World Wide Fund for Nature's global conservation effort.

A new campaign to preserve the thin strip of lush forest, which once covered 1 million square kilometres but has been 98 per cent destroyed by man's encroachments, is jerking Brazilians into awareness that some of the country's environmental treasures are found in a coastal strip stretching from Recife in the north-east to São Paulo in the south.

The WWF, which has been donating money for conservation in the Amazon and Atlantic forest regions since 1979, plans to spend

Woolly spider monkey

about $1m (£550,000) a year on Brazil. It recently made a $200,000

From Richard House in São Paulo

gift, part of which will be used to set up forest posts to keep illegal hunters and squatters out of the reserves.

The broken range of hills and cliffs along Brazil's eastern seaboard acts as a sponge for the warm, rain-heavy clouds sweeping off the Atlantic. In the drippingly-fertile forests live 20,000 plant species and 21 different primates, 17 of them unique to Brazil. Yet all but two of these apes are endangered species. The Atlantic forest includes the built-up tourist riviera between Rio and São Paulo, and areas badly affected by industrial pollution which also suffer from illegal logging and invasion by squatters.

The golden lion tamarin is a tiny, carrot-coloured monkey weighing less than a pound. Only about 400 tamarins survive in Brazil's forests – fewer than the total number in zoos around the world.

But the star of Latin America's primates is the woolly spider monkey or muriqui, of which no more than 300 are believed to exist. It is the continent's largest ape. Locally, the muriqui, which weighs about 45 lb, eats leaves and shoots and swings by its tail through the trees, has replaced the Chinese panda as the symbol of conservation.

There are some 50 parks and reserves on the Atlantic seaboard, four inhabited by the muriqui.

Forest Ecosystems 31

The Coniferous Forestry Industry in Sweden

Sweden, like other developed countries with large areas of coniferous forest (e.g. Canada, Finland), has a low population density and faces none of the acute problems of rainforest areas. Information on the coniferous forest ecosystem was given on page 29; 5.13 gives details of forestry in Sweden.

The National Forest Enterprise in Sweden (which is run by the government), and private forest owners, manage the forest resource very carefully. In fact the amount of forest in Sweden is actually increasing. When a stand of trees matures, it is cut and must be replanted within three years. About 2000 container-grown trees are planted in each hectare. The young trees are sometimes fertilised with nitrates (often spread from the air) but the amount used is carefully regulated to prevent excessive wash-off into water sources. When the stands are 2–3 metres high they are thinned. At maturity, trees are cut down and transported (mainly by lorry) to processing plants where many of the products (sawn timber, pulp, paper and board products) are exported to other developed countries.

In all stages of production, from planting to saw mill, machines are heavily used; the number of workers is falling while output is rising. The Swedish government has the money and organisation to ensure that the forest resource is properly managed for the benefit of present and future generations. All forests are used for recreation, and 20 National Parks have been set up. Research is carried out into all aspects of forestry by universities and government departments, and there are 26 secondary schools offering specialised forestry courses.

What lessons, if any, do you think developing countries with rainforests can learn from countries like Sweden?

▼ 5.13 Forestry in Sweden

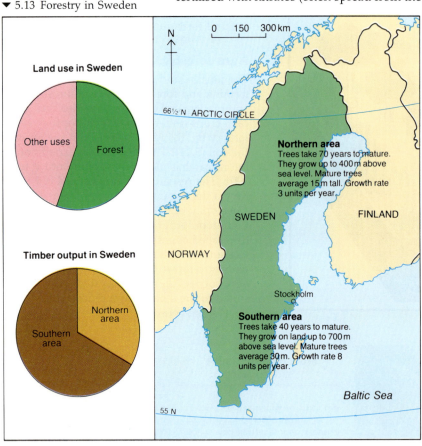

Coniferous Forest in Britain

Much of Britain was once covered with a natural vegetation of broadleaf deciduous forest including trees such as oak and ash. For over 2000 years more and more forest was gradually cleared and very little now remains. Throughout this century replanting of trees (**afforestation**) has taken place. The Government-controlled Forestry Commission have done most of the replanting, mainly with non-native conifer trees. There has been a 300% increase in forest area since 1947, the largest increase being in upland Scotland. The reasons for afforestation are:

- to reduce Britain's dependence on imported timber;
- to enable some money to be made from low-quality land;
- to slow down the rain run-off in water catchment areas.

Many people are concerned about the impact of afforested areas because they only support a restricted range of plant and animal life. The scale of the concern can be appreciated when it is realised that over 50% of the heath, moorland and upland areas in Britain are forested or likely to be forested with conifers.

Look carefully at 5.14a and b. 5.14a shows a traditional forest road. 5.14b shows how the roadside can be changed to attract a greater range of plant and animal life. Describe and explain what has been done.

▼ 5.14 Enhancement of lowland forest roadsides

▲ 5.15 Deciduous (broadleaf) woodland

Deciduous Woodlands in Britain

Unlike planted coniferous forests, deciduous woodlands (5.15) are not generally economically valuable for timber production. A survey of ownership and uses of deciduous woodland in Wales (5.16) tells us much about the current situation, and 5.17 gives a generally positive picture about the attitudes of the main owners: the farmers. There is increasing general concern about the loss of deciduous woodland that is still taking place. Unlike the coniferous forest, the deciduous wood in Britain is very rich in bird, animal, insect and plant life. In addition, most people agree that deciduous woodland is beautiful, with its variety of tree size, shape and colour. Broadleaved trees are disappearing faster than they are being replaced because of:

- pressure to build more houses in the countryside,
- woods and hedges being uprooted to clear the way for agricultural machines,
- road-building programmes.

Britain has a surplus of cereals, dairy products and meat which means that some farmers are looking at alternative uses for their land. Deciduous woods on farms could become a valuable source of timber as well as being used for shelter and recreation. There are grants and tax concessions available to farmers who wish to treat deciduous woods as a major farm resource.

But many people feel that the speed of change is too slow. 5.18 gives information about the Woodland Trust, the only conservation group concerned solely with saving broadleaved woods.

Make a simple survey of woodland/forest in your area. What sort of trees are found and how are they managed? Can you suggest any action to improve the woodland/forest?

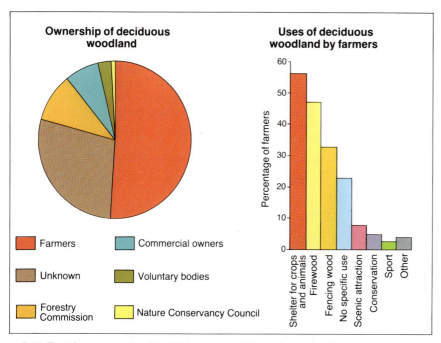

▲ 5.16 Deciduous woodland in Wales: ownership and uses by farmers

Attitude	Woods/trees in general	Landscape	Wildlife	Game	Financial gain/loss
Strongly interested/ appreciative/anxious	12	10	10	—	7
Quite interested/ appreciative/anxious	13	16	14	8	9
Mildly interested/ appreciative/anxious	6	4	5	8	5
Indifferent/against	4	5	6	19	14

▲ 5.17 Attitudes of Welsh farmers to deciduous woodland

▼ 5.18 The Woodland Trust

THE WOODLAND TRUST IN ACTION

This is what the Woodland Trust is doing to preserve our countryside.
- The Trust purchases and maintains woods in danger.
- We protect other areas by accepting woodland and land for tree planting as gifts. This relieves owners from considerable management responsibilities.
- We create new broadleaved woods by planting.
- Professional staff organise specialist care of our trees and woods. Just a few full-time staff run Woodland Rescue, our national fundraising campaign.
- We provide woods for you to enjoy.
- The Trust gives shelter to birds, animals and plants that might otherwise disappear, by conserving and creating woodland.

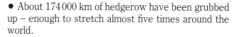

Since 1947, in England and Wales . . .
- 40% of broadleaved woodland has disappeared.
- More than half of our ancient woodland has been destroyed or has fallen into neglect.
- Conifer plantations increased from 104 000 hectares in 1947 to 426 000 hectares in 1980.
- About 174 000 km of hedgerow have been grubbed up – enough to stretch almost five times around the world.

And . . .
- Hedgerow loss increased to 6400 km a year in the 1980's.
- Over 20 million elm trees have been killed by Dutch elm disease.
- In Scotland, less than 1% of the trees planted in 1985 were broadleaved species.

Forest Ecosystems 33

6 Desertification

Key ideas
- Drought is an increasing problem in many parts of the world.
- The reasons for increasing drought are complex, but may be largely the result of human activities, rather than natural processes.

There are reports from around the world that the climate is changing and that deserts are expanding. **Desertification** is the process by which an area loses its vegetation cover, leading to the destruction of soil fertility and eventually to a barren desert.

The United Nations statistics on the effect of desertification seem frightening.
- Each year 21 million hectares (about the size of the UK) of productive soils are impoverished by desertification to a level at which no food can be produced.
- Desertification costs $26 billion each year in lost food production.
- Between 1958 and 1975 the Sahara Desert grew southwards by an average of about 6 km per year. In 1989 US President Bush, speaking about the need to give the area aid, suggested that it was now growing at 9 km per year.

6.1 shows that the problem is not just African. *Use an atlas to help you to describe the areas that are at risk.*

However, a number of scientists now question some of the UN's statistics. A major problem is that no-one is really sure what the 'normal' climate of these areas is. Most of the countries only have weather records going back 50 years. It is therefore possible that what we are now seeing is more 'normal' than the weather of 10, 20 or 30 years ago.

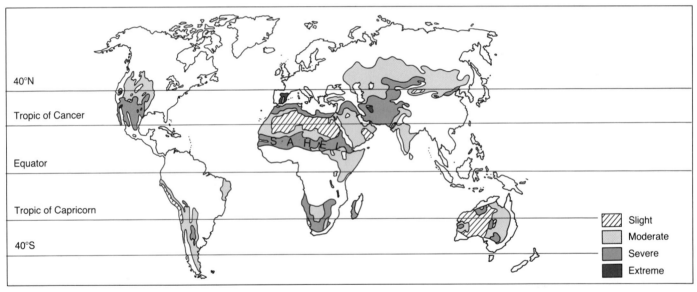

▲ 6.1 Areas at risk from desertification

▼ 6.2 Desertification in the Sahel

It is also important to remember that the rainfall in **semi-arid** areas (areas at the edges of deserts) is always very variable and unreliable. It is quite usual for an area with an average annual precipitation of 350 mm to have years when there is less than 150 mm or more than 550 mm. Reports of drought from a semi-arid area are only to be expected if two or three years of below-average rainfall come together. It does not necessarily mean that there has been a change in the climate.

There is increasing evidence that short-term droughts may be due to changes in the surface temperatures of the sea. The 1988 drought in central USA has been linked to exceptionally cold water in the tropical Pacific Ocean. Studies of weather records have also shown that years of low rainfall in the Sahel region of Africa (6.1) occur when differences in temperature between the oceans of the northern and southern hemisphere are particularly large. This information has allowed accurate forecasts of probable rainfall to be made up to several months in advance.

The only region of the world where there is any solid evidence that rainfall is falling below normal levels is the northern more-arid part of the Sahel. Here much land that was productive in the 1960s and 1970s is now little more than barren waste (6.2). Elsewhere desertification is largely the result of an increasing number of people trying to live off the meagre water resources of semi-arid lands. In order to survive they often have little choice but to use unsuitable farming methods. As a result both the water and land resources suffer.

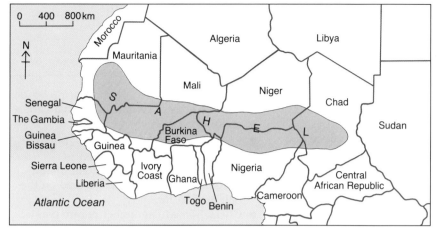

▲ 6.3 The Sahel

▼ 6.4 Cash crops: the ruin of the Sahel

The Sahel

6.3 shows the countries of the Sahel. The northern half of the zone has an annual precipitation of less than 350 mm, and experienced lower than average rainfall for much of the 1970s and 1980s. In the southern half, with an annual precipitation of 350–750 mm, there has been a great variation in rainfall, but no evidence of an overall decline.

However, during the 1970s and 1980s tens of thousands of people died throughout the Sahel as a result of a lack of water. The reasons for this are complex (and include a long civil war), but undoubtedly high population growth played an important part, and also a drive to grow cash crops, often in areas suited only to nomadic herding. There was extensive overgrazing and, after vegetation was removed, the structure of the soil broke down and erosion took place. As soil is blown around there is an increasing number of dust storms, and there is evidence that this has reduced rainfall and worsened the situation. *Outline the changes in land-use shown in 6.4, and describe their effects.*

Traditionally the farmers of the Sahel lived in harmony with each other and the environment. The farmers of the south grew millet and sorghum, with areas between villages left fallow. The nomadic herders grazed their animals in the northern Sahel during the wet season (b), but retreated to the south in the dry season (a). Here they received millet and sorghum from the southern farmers, and land to graze their cattle, in return for animal products and fertilisation of the land.

However, during the 1950s and 1960s the fallow areas were increasingly used to grow cash crops, especially peanuts (c). The nomads were deprived of grazing land in the dry season, and the sedentary farmers no longer received natural fertiliser. Peanut growing was eventually also extended into the drier areas previously used only by the nomads (d).

▼ 6.5 Aralsk, USSR

Aralsk: the Port without a Sea

Until the 1960s Aralsk was the most important port on the Aral Sea, a large inland sea in the USSR. It had a large fishing fleet and was quite prosperous. The Aral Sea was fed by two large rivers, the Syr Darya and Amu Darya, which rise in the mountains to the south-east.

However, in a very large irrigation scheme to produce cash crops, particularly cotton, in Uzbekistan, large quantities of water have been removed from the two rivers before they enter the sea. The effect has been catastrophic. So much water has been removed that the level of the sea has fallen by over 12 metres. In places the shore line has retreated by more than 50 km, and much of the dried-up sea bed has become a salty wilderness. Aralsk is no longer on the shores of the sea, and the fishing boats lie high and dry (6.5).

There is also evidence of increasing aridity with reduced rainfall in the area around the sea. 'Salt-storms' are common, with salt being blown up to 500 km, ruining good agricultural land.

7 Coastal Management

Key ideas
- A variety of ecosystems can be found at coasts, all of which are finely balanced and easily disturbed.
- There are often conflicts between different human uses of coastal areas.
- Effective management of the coast is vital.

Coasts are constantly changing as a result of natural processes and human activities. These changes have helped to produce a wide variety of ecosystems which, like the coasts themselves, constantly change (7.1).

The natural processes affecting the coast are complex, but three major factors must be considered.

- Is the level of the sea relative to the land rising or falling? If the sea is rising, the land may be drowned whereas, if it is falling, new land will appear.
- Is the coast being **eroded** (worn away) or is material being **deposited** (laid down). Cliffs are often a sign of coastal erosion and beaches a sign of coastal deposition.
- In what direction is material (sand and shingle) being moved along the coast? Eroded material may stay close to the cliff from which it came, but often it is moved by **longshore drift** (page 37) along the coast to form such features as beaches and spits. Silt brought down by rivers may be deposited in an estuary, push out new land into the sea, or be moved along the coast.

These processes have resulted in a variety of ecosystems.

- **Estuaries**: covered with water at high tide; at low tide vast expanses of mudbanks, sandbanks and salt-marsh appear. Many types of birds feed on the rich marine life.
- **Cliffs**: home to a number of rare plants, and nesting place for many sea birds.
- **Dunes**: contain rare plants, insects, animals and birds.
- **Lagoons and marshlands**: rapidly diminishing in number as areas are drained. Contain many rare plants, insects, animals and birds.
- **Open water**: water of different depths contains different species of plants and fish, which in turn provide food for birds and mammals.

All of these ecosystems are under threat of destruction by human activities; and many species of coastal insects, birds, mammals and plants are in danger of extinction. 7.1 shows some examples.

Look at 7.1. In what ways do any of the human activities shown endanger the coastal ecosystems? In what ways do the various human activities conflict with each other?

▼ 7.1 Coastal ecosystems

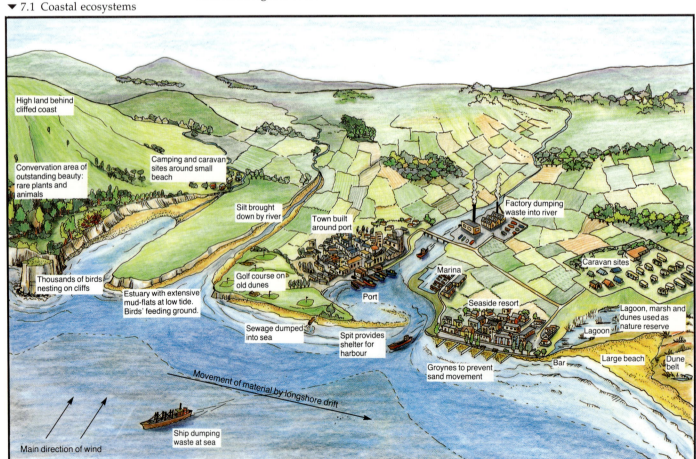

▲ 7.2 Longshore drift

▼ 7.4 Sandy shore and mobile dunes

▼ 7.5 Mudflats and saltmarsh

▼ 7.6 Marram grass planting

▼ 7.7 Reinforcement of dunes as protection from human use

Dawlish Warren

Dawlish Warren Nature Reserve in Devon is centred on a sand spit over 2 km long. It is joined to the mainland at its western end and extends into the mouth of the River Exe, providing shelter for the port of Exmouth.

The spit is made of material which has been moved by longshore drift from an area further west where sandstone cliffs are being eroded. The dominant south-westerly winds make the waves break at an angle to the coast. The material is pushed up the beach at this angle by the **swash**, but returns downslope in the **backswash**, resulting in a drift up the coast (7.2). Eventually the sand is deposited, forming a spit.

7.3 shows the variety of habitats within the reserve.

- **Sandy shore**: the area between high and low water which may be attractive to holiday makers, but is a very hostile place for plants and animals. Few can adapt to the unstable conditions with its extremes of temperature and changing water conditions (7.4).
- **Mobile dunes**: where sand is still building up, trapped by marram grass, the most important plant for fixing sand. Its tough leaves trap wind-blown sand, while its extensive root system binds the sand preventing it from blowing away (7.4).
- **Fixed dunes**: where sand is no longer being blown onto the land, so conditions are more stable and plants other than marram can colonise. The soil is dry, sandy, lacks nutrients and tends to be acidic, favouring some specialised plant species, especially heathers and gorse.
- **Mudflats**: although these appear to be barren of life, they are one of the most productive environments on earth. Conditions are very harsh, but animals which have adapted have a rich supply of food washed down by the river and brought in by the sea. Some idea of just how many animals live in the mud can be gained by seeing the thousands of wading birds which feed there (7.5).

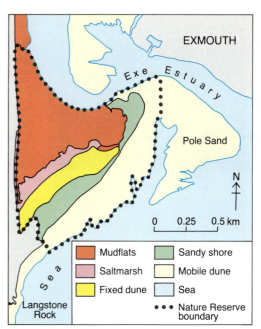

▲ 7.3 Dawlish Warren

- **Saltmarsh**: the upper reaches of the mudflats, which the tide covers least often, have been colonised by plants able to survive wet salty conditions. The type of plant depends largely on the length of time the area is exposed by the tide. Eel-grass and certain algae thrive at the lower fringe; cord-grass, sea rush and sea lavender are common on the high reaches (7.5).

The reserve also contains smaller areas of reedbeds, scrub, fresh-water ponds and wet grassland, each with their own animal and plant communities.

Part of the management of the reserve involves conserving and enhancing the various habitats. The dunes are of crucial importance, and in places they become damaged and eroded by holiday makers and have to be fenced off to allow replanting to take place (7.6). At the western edge of the spit, human erosion has become so great that mobile dunes have been reinforced with concrete and rock (7.7).

Sand dunes are in many ways better than sea walls at protecting the coast from sea erosion and flooding.

- Dunes absorb wave energy; walls cannot.
- If a breach occurs, flooding over the dunes is usually gradual and shallow, whereas with walls it is likely to be sudden and deep.
- A series of dune ridges is better protection than just one wall.
- Dunes with vegetation can build themselves up, whereas walls cannot.
- Dunes are a much broader barrier than walls.

Dawlish Warren is a popular holiday resort. What management opportunities and problems will visitors to Dawlish Warren create?

Coastal Management

ON THE BRINK

Centimetres away from plunging into the sea, a family's home perches on the brink of a crumbling cliff. Erosion by the sea has steadily brought more than 40 homes in the picturesque village of Fairlight Cover, near Hastings in East Sussex, nearer and nearer to disaster. Five houses were abandoned when they became unsafe. One man managed to save his home by using rollers to move it inland.

But in August 1989 villagers finally won a three-year battle to persuade the local council to save their homes. At first Rother Council refused to help, claiming that preservation work would cost more than the homes were worth. However, they have now decided to spend £2 million on a concrete barrier to protect the cliffs from further erosion after villagers proved their houses were worth £3 million.

▲ 7.8 On the brink

Sea Erosion

There are three main ways in which land is eroded by the sea (7.8).

- **Hydraulic action**: as waves pound rocks, air is trapped in cracks; when waves retreat, air expands violently and breaks off bits of rock.
- **Abrasion**: rock fragments are thrown at the foot of the cliffs by waves, and bits of the cliff are eroded; the size of these fragments is then reduced when they bang together and break (**attrition**).
- **Solution**: some rocks, such as chalk and limestone, are slowly dissolved by sea water.

All three types of erosion cause **undercutting** of cliffs (7.9). Weaknesses in the rock, such as cracks or joints, are picked out by the sea, making the cliff line uneven and producing caves in some types of rock. Continuous undercutting will cause the cliff to collapse, and as this happens again and again a **wave-cut platform** is left behind. In time, waves lose much of their energy in crossing the widening platform and so cliff erosion slows down, or even stops completely. When waves attack a headland from both sides, or where lines of weakness are picked out by wave action, **arches** may form. If the roof of the arch collapses, a **stack** is left.

The rate of erosion depends on the following.

- The force of the waves: most erosion is carried out during storms.
- The hardness of the rock: cliffs made of soft rocks such as clay erode much faster than cliffs of harder rock such as granite.
- The depth of water offshore: if the water is very shallow, waves may lose much of their power before they reach the cliffs.
- The power of the tide in reinforcing the force of waves and moving loosened material.

Protecting a coastline from erosion can be very difficult and costly. The value of dunes was noted on page 37, but these occur in relatively few locations. Sometimes a sea wall made of concrete is built out from the shore (7.10). In other areas, to break the power of the waves, large boulders are dumped at the base of a cliff, and in some places boulders are used in front of sea walls (7.11). Artificial beaches can also be created, usually by dumping thousands of tonnes of gravel and sand on the wave-cut platform. The aim here is to weaken the waves' power before they reach the cliffs.

Whatever solution is used, once built, sea defences have to be checked and reinforced constantly. A single violent storm may destroy years of work.

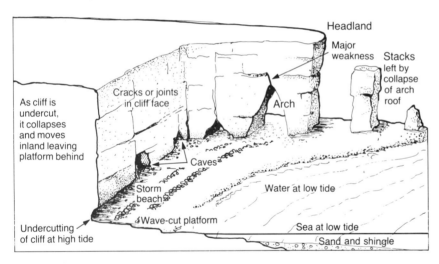

▲ 7.9 Coastal erosion

▼ 7.10 Sea wall at Lyme Regis

▼ 7.11 Sea defences at Arromanche, Normandy

Look at 7.12. In your own words outline each of the three incidents described, and the causes of the problem in each case. Find newspaper articles of your own about coastal pollution and make a list of the ways in which coasts are damaged. Suggest ways in which some of the problems could be solved.

▼ 7.12 *Today*, 18 July 1989

Sea, Sand and Sewage

The Marine Conservation Society suggests that we often get a free 'gift' with every seaside holiday: disgusting sewage pollution, which not only smells and looks nasty but is also damaging our health. And it is not only sewage that could make a visit to a holiday beach an unpleasant experience; 7.12 shows just some of the problems that might be found on a Mediterranean beach holiday.

The European Community (EC) does set limits as to what can be considered a safe bathing beach, in terms of the amount of sewage and litter. However, these limits allow ten times as much sewage as Canada's standards do. In Canada, when sea water has one-fifth of the sewage allowed by European standards, public health authorities have to post notices on the beach, warning bathers that they risk health problems such as diarrhoea and throat or ear infections if they swim.

Yet, even with the EC's lax standards, almost half of Britain's 369 official bathing beaches failed to comply, and a number had more than 40 times the permitted amount of sewage. Among those that failed were some of the most popular seaside resorts, including Blackpool, Brighton, Morecambe and Scarborough.

£1 billion will have to be spent on improving Britain's bathing beaches by 1995 if they are to meet the European standards, and this will have to be paid for either by higher water charges, or by taxes.

SCUM ON IN... THE WATER'S FILTHY

THE stench of decay made your stomach churn a full 50 feet away.

What used to be sparkling blue sea had been turned into a dappled grey mess, as if someone had thrown a few million gallons of wallpaper paste into the ocean.

Although the 60 miles of Rimini beach was packed with tourists, many of them British, no one dared to take a dip. *No one, that is, except me.*

As people stared in disbelief, I waded into water thick with rotting algae, a creeping, stinking menace which has ruined this once glorious stretch of the Italian Riviera — and thousands of holidays with it.

I emerged, looking something like the creature from the black lagoon and desperately in need of a shower.

But for thousands of British sun-seekers, the nightmare won't wash away.

Not only have their holidays been spoiled, but compensation has been ruled out by tourist chiefs who deny that the algae spread has been worsened by pollution in the Adriatic.

The slime, which emerged more than a week ago, is caused by rotting algae which has risen to the surface of the Adriatic because of increased sea temperatures.

Tourist chiefs, who cater for 300,000 British holidaymakers a year, fear it could spell disaster for their trade.

They have been given £50 million by the government to try to wipe out the menace.

Raw sewage bars children from the sea

MAJORCA

BRITISH holidaymakers in Majorca are being driven from beaches by the stench of raw sewage.

Families forbid their disappointed children from swimming in the murky sea, while people who do venture in have emerged covered in a sticky brown tar-like substance.

"I hope it was tar because the other thing it looked like is too awful to think about," said London secretary Kay Stirling, who spent two weeks at an apartment near Cala D'Or.

"You can see what looks like sewage pipes 200 yards out, pumping stuff into the sea at night."

The island's tourist chiefs have launched a £37 million clean-up to stop holidaymakers deserting the beaches.

By the end of summer, work will have begun on new sewage treatment plants at Muro, Santa Margarita, Arta, Calas de Mallorca, Cala Murada and Cala D'Or.

The three-year campaign will also include neighbouring sunshine islands Ibiza and Menorca.

GREEK GLORY BURIED UNDER LITTER

RHODES

FROM the hilltop, St Paul's Bay glistened like a jewel at the foot of towering Lindos Acropolis on the Greek island of Rhodes.

To Sarah White and Tony Lyons, from Dorset, the scene was just as it appeared in the guide books.

But as they descended the steep path to one of the Mediterranean's most famous beauty spots, swarms of flies and scattered rubbish dominated their view.

On the path, a rusting bin spilled weeks-old debris.

At the beach, near where children played and couples sunbathed, half-empty oil cans, drinks tins, discarded fruit, torn bin liners and other litter spoiled the narrow crescent of sand.

"The bay looked fabulous from the top of the hill," says Tony, 33. "But this is a tragedy.

"The rubbish spoils a beautiful scene. It obviously hasn't been cleared for weeks.

"Some of it, like the oil cans, looks as though it was washed up from the sea, while the rest has just been discarded by dirty people. The heat makes it particularly nasty," he adds.

8 Wetlands

Key ideas
- The wetlands of the world provide some of the richest natural habitats for wildlife of all kinds.
- Wetlands are being lost to development at an increasingly rapid pace.

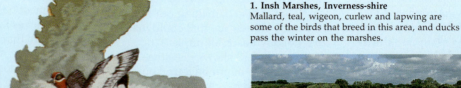

1. Insh Marshes, Inverness-shire
Mallard, teal, wigeon, curlew and lapwing are some of the birds that breed in this area, and ducks pass the winter on the marshes.

2. Leighton Moss, Lancashire
The reedbeds of Leighton Moss provide a northern outpost for bittern and bearded tit – and possibly marsh harriers. The Moss also has otters.

3. Jeffry Bog, Yorkshire
This SSSI is rich in plant life, including wild angelica, marsh marigold and ragged-robin.

4. Strangford Lough
This 1000-acre site is an intertidal area where many fresh-water streams converge and flowering eel grass abounds. It is a wintering ground for many waterfowl.

5. Shotwick Brook, Cheshire
This area of low-lying pasture is an important roosting site for waders including the black-tailed godwit, dunlin, golden plover and lapwing.

6. Ty'n y Maes and Ty Gwyn Farms, Gwynedd
These two farms occupy a large part of the spectacular glaciated valley of the River Ogwen. Purple moorgrass, tufted hairgrass, brown bent, bog-mosses and orchids abound.

7. Norfolk Broads
These contain a rich variety of lakes, swamps, waterways and marshes. Rare plants and birds flourish.

8. Ouse Washes, Cambridgeshire
This is the largest area of regularly flooded freshwater grazing marsh in the country. It has huge concentrations of wildfowl making it an internationally important area. It also provides a breeding area for duck and rare waders.

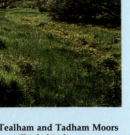

11. Tealham and Tadham Moors
Otters still inhabit these moors, which also contain some of the most interesting bird and plant life on the Somerset Levels.

12. Exminster Marshes, Devon
Large numbers of wigeon, ringed plover, black-tailed godwit and dark-bellied brent geese and avocet winter here.

13. Troublefield, Dorset
This wetland is rich in vegetation including herbs such as yellow flag and meadowsweet. Eighteen species of dragonfly and damselfly, and many woodland birds can also be found.

10. Oare Marshes, Kent
The Oare Marshes are one of the most valuable wildlife habitats in Kent. Birds such as yellow wagtail, snipe and redshank breed here. The area is also rich in plant life.

9. Old Hall Marshes, Essex
This site on the Blackwater estuary is the main breeding ground for wildfowl on the Essex coast.

40 Wetlands

8.1 shows some of the major wetland areas of the UK where the World Wide Fund for Nature has been active in saving wildlife. Make a list of the different types of habitat shown. For each type list the animals and plants that rely upon it.

Are wetlands worth saving? Discuss the arguments both for and against.

▼ 8.2 Lake Ichkeul, Tunisia

Using the text and map, identify the different habitats that can be found in and around the lake. What pressures on animals and plants are shown on the map? Do you think that such schemes as this should be allowed?

▼ 8.3 Lake Ichkeul

Wetlands are the most productive – and most threatened – ecosystems. The marshes, swamps and flood plains upon which were founded the civilisations of ancient Egypt, Mesopotamia and Indo-China, and which continue today to support rural communities throughout the world, are menaced by drainage, reclamation and pollution.

(Dr Monkombu S Swaminathan, President of the World Wide Fund for Nature (WWF) in India.)

There are many different kinds of wetlands, but they all have in common that they are often waterlogged. They can be thought of as neither land nor sea, neither wet nor dry. Yet they support a rich variety of animals and plants.

Wetlands are under threat throughout the world.

- Drainage schemes are used to dry out the wetlands so that more intensive farming can be introduced.
- Reclamation schemes dry out areas that were once part of a sea, lake or river, leaving 'new' land available for a wide variety of uses.
- River management schemes control the flow of rivers artificially, changing water levels in rivers, lakes and seas, with the result that wetland areas often dry out.
- Logging, particularly of mangrove forest, can destroy the wetland habitat.
- Polluted water draining into a wetland area can seriously damage plant, insect and animal life.
- Harbour and port development schemes may require waterways to be dredged, and wetland to be dug out to make harbours or marinas.

Approximately 6% of the world's land surface is covered with wetlands and, because of concern about their loss, organisations such as the World Wide Fund for Nature are working throughout the world to protect them. Over 50 countries have now joined the **Ramsar Convention**, which is an international agreement to stem the loss of wetlands now and in the future. They have listed 421 particularly valuable sites, covering almost 30 million hectares, which are to be specially protected.

Lake Ichkeul

Lake Ichkeul National Park (8.2, 8.3) is located in northern Tunisia. It is one of the most important wetland sites for waterfowl in the world, the first to be on three international conservation lists, being named as a **Biosphere Reserve, Ramsar Site, and World Heritage Site.**

It is somewhat surprising to find a huge lake in a country which is largely desert. Lake Ichkeul and its surrounding marshes cover 130 km^2. Its position on the southern side of the Mediterranean makes it particularly important as a wintering ground for waterfowl that breed in Europe and Siberia, and travel south to take advantage of the mild climate. During winter up to 150 000 birds can be found in and around the lake, mostly coot, wigeon and pochard. Lying near a coastline which has few mudflats and feeding grounds, the lake is a welcome resting ground.

Whereas most wetlands consist of large flat expanses of marshes, at Ichkeul the mountains lie along the south side of the lake, and rise directly out of the marsh, creating a very dramatic landscape. Dominated by olive and pistachio woodland, and with numerous limestone cliffs, the mountains support many typical Mediterranean birds. The mountains are also an important nesting ground for eight species of birds of prey, including Egyptian vultures and Lanner falcons.

Ichkeul's greatest asset is that it is a permanent lake: it never dries out. As winter approaches, the rains begin, and seasonal rivers bring fresh water into the lake. This raises the level of the lake and flushes out the salt which has built up during the hot dry summer.

Survival of the rich ecosystem is dependent on rainfall and sea water being mixed to provide the correct conditions. Tunisia is a rapidly developing country and the government wants to increase its water supplies by damming a number of the rivers that feed the lake. Without this fresh water, the lake's salinity would increase rapidly, to up to twice that of sea water, turning this thriving wetland into a virtually 'dead' sea. The Tunisian government is attempting to reduce the impact of its plans, but the danger of permanent damage being done to the lake remains.

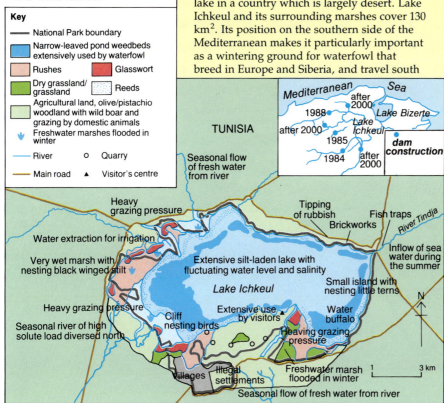

9 The Need for Land

Key ideas
- There are many different demands for land which vary from area to area and through time.
- Careful management is essential if all the demands are to be adequately met.

Land is perhaps *the* most basic resource for much of human activity and we are increasingly aware that the amount of land available, like many other resources, is finite and should not be wasted.
Look at 9.1 which shows some of the major uses of land in the UK. (It is most unlikely these would all occur together in such a small area!) Make a list of all the different uses shown.

Getting the Most from Land

When the amount of land available for human activity is limited, people try to get the most from the land. In the centre of urban areas (9.2), land is in great demand, so high-rise development is usually used to give the maximum amount of floor space from the minimum of ground space.

Where land for agriculture is limited, crops are grown intensively. For example, more crops can be grown by terracing hillsides (9.3). As the number of people in the world increases, and the variety of their activities increases, so the effective management of land becomes increasingly urgent.

▲ 9.2 High-rise development

▼ 9.3 Intensive farming

▼ 9.1 Major land uses in the UK

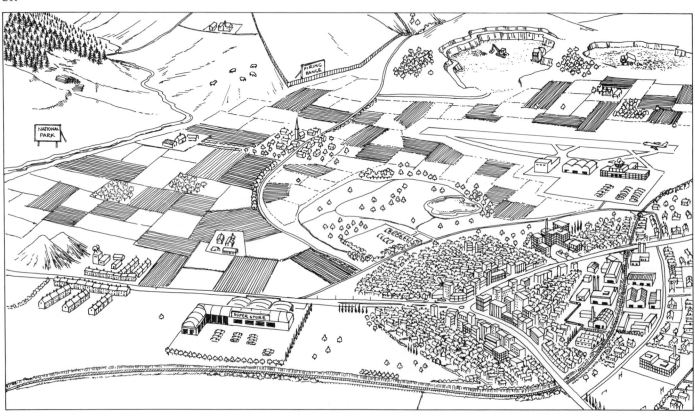

42 The Need for Land

▲ 9.4 Derelict (old industrial) land

The Problem of Dereliction

Derelict land is land which has been damaged by human activity or neglected so that it cannot be used to its full potential. In this unit we look at dereliction which is the result of industrial activity, found in many developed countries such as the UK.

9.4 shows an old demolished steel works in Wales, which clearly illustrates how unsightly derelict land is. Derelict land can also be unsafe, and 9.5 gives information about these two aspects of the problem within the UK as a whole. In the 1970s and 1980s the widespread decline of heavy industry created a large number of derelict sites. Steel works were particularly heavily hit, as were old coal mining areas. Changes in transport systems have meant that disused railway land is a common feature in many urban areas. Docklands which are far from the open sea and cannot handle large modern ships have also been severely affected. It is now accepted that this deserted land cannot be left as wasteland: **reclamation** must take place so that the land can be used again. At the same time, it is important to prevent future dereliction. Much attention has been given to the problems of dereliction in Britain's inner cities, but some people are becoming increasingly concerned that run-down council estates farther out from the city centres are equally in need of action.

What is being done?

The UK government and the EC offer financial help towards the reclamation of derelict land. Usually the money is used to develop the area for new industry or commerce, rather than to form areas of 'green' open space.

The main UK initiatives for reclamation and development of derelict land are as follows.

- *Derelict Land Grant* available in areas of heavy dereliction. Local authorities obtain 100% of the cost of reclamation and private landowners over 80%.
- *Urban Regeneration Grant* available in urban areas to private property owners who own large sites in need of redevelopment to provide new jobs.
- *Urban Programme* available to turn derelict factories into small factory units for new businesses.
- *Urban Development Corporation Grant* available in areas of great dereliction where the whole infrastructure (roads, etc.) needs replacing.

In addition many local authorities and local business people put up money themselves to tackle dereliction.

9.6 shows how various sources of money are being used to reclaim derelict land alongside the Leeds–Liverpool Canal.

▼ 9.6 Leeds–Liverpool canal corridor

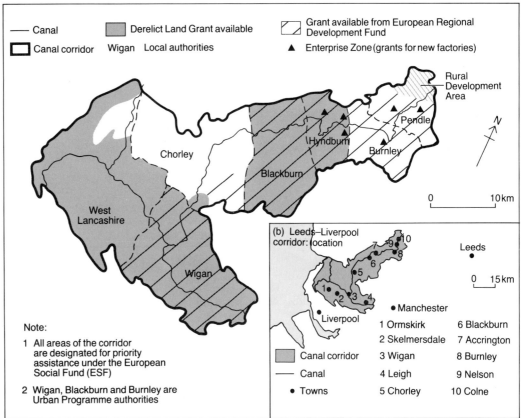

▼ 9.5 Characteristics of derelict land, UK

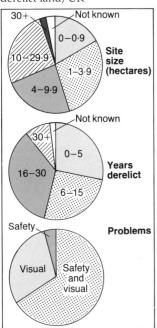

The Need for Land

▶ 9.7 Uses for reclaimed derelict land
(a) Housing
(b) Industry
(c) Amenity

Uses of Derelict Land

Much derelict land is found close to where people live. Children are at risk when playing near abandoned factories, shafts or canals. Rubbish is often tipped onto derelict land and attracts vermin, which creates a health hazard. But *most important* is that derelict land gives the nearby area a neglected and run-down atmosphere which can cause local people to lose respect for their environment (and themselves) and lead to further dereliction. Unsightly wasteland can drive residents, workers and established industries away to more attractive places, and at the same time it discourages new industries and residents from coming to the area.

Land reclamation can transform derelict land into useful new land to serve the needs of development and to improve the environment. This means more land for homes, for jobs and for amenity use (9.7a–c). By using derelict land in the ways shown in 9.7 *valuable* land can be saved from development. Valuable has many meanings:

- expensive to buy and build on;
- valuable for other economic activities such as agriculture;
- valuable for the quality of its wildlife or for general recreational use.

It is the last meaning that is increasingly important to many people and why the pressure to re-use derelict land to the full is growing.

Using a spoil heap

Spoil heaps or 'tips' of waste from activities like coal mining are a common sight in many parts of Britain. Coal tips form a scar on the landscape and present dangers of many kinds. The tip material is generally not suitable to build on so these areas are often reclaimed for leisure/amenity use. 9.8 shows what can be done. Vegetation is often sparse or lacking on tips but any established tree or scrub communities are usually saved to act as sources for the spread of seeds, insects and animals.

Tip heaps are often landscaped during reclamation to remove steep slopes or high points, and this can make them look 'new' for many years. Attempts to create a 'mature' appearance by transplanting large trees are not always successful, and large trees are also very expensive. So usually the smaller trees are planted because they cost less and have a greater chance of success. Many coal tips are close to areas of old terraced houses and when reclaimed the tips form valuable areas of open space and recreation for the local community.

Look carefully at 9.8 and try to explain why the various uses were sited at the particular places marked.

Afteruse

Deciding on the **afteruse** of a derelict area is a complex business. 9.9 gives details of the economic value of the various uses, obviously a very important consideration. 9.10 gives information about the different requirements of the afteruses.

▶ 9.8 Former spoil heap, reclaimed for leisure use

44 The Need for Land

Requirements:

Afteruses

	Flat areas (1:50)	Large area (5 ha)	Varied slopes	Open water or streams	Stable soils	Road access	Nearness to services	Urban location	Countryside location: general	Countryside location: National Park AONB	Money to develop	Return on investment	Intensive long-term management	Special long-term management	Mixture of habitats	Fertile soil	Infertile soil	Trees	Shrubs	Productive grassland	Rough grass
Industry	●	●	□	■	●	●	○	●	□	■	●	●						○	○		
Housing	●	○	○	□	●	●	●	●	○	□	●	●				○	□	○	○		
Agriculture																					
cultivation	◆	○	□					◆	○		○	●	●	●	□	●	■				
productive grazing		○							○		○	●	○			○	□	◆	◆	●	
marginal grazing		◆							○			◆	●								
allotments	○					◆	◆	●			●	●			●						
Forestry																					
commercial		●							●			●	●		●		●			□	□
marginal		○							○			●	●		◆		●		◆		
Recreation Intensive																					
sport	○	◆	◆/■			◆		○			●	●	○	○		○	◆			○	◆
picnic sites	◆		◆	◆		●			○	○	◆				◆			○	○		◆
camp sites	○	◆	○			●	○	◆	○	○	○	○						○	○	◆	
car parks	◆	□	□	■	○	●	◆									●	◆				
Recreation Extensive																					
casual/public open space		◆	○	◆				●	◆						○		◆	●	●		●
Wildlife																					
casual/education		◆	●	○					●	◆				◆	○		○	●	●		●
nature conservation education				●	○					◆	●	◆					○	●	●		●

○ desirable   ● necessary   □ desirable (could be modified)   ■ impossible   ◆ useful (in some cases)

▲ 9.10 Land requirements for various afteruses

Look carefully at 9.11 which shows a disused railway track leading to a derelict quarry. The area is quite close to an urban area. All afteruses except agriculture and forestry are theoretically possible for the area. *Describe and explain how you would reclaim the area and make a labelled sketch of what the area might look like when your reclamation is complete.*

▼ 9.11 Disused quarry and mineral line

▼ 9.9 Afteruses of derelict sites

Afteruse	Economic value
Industry Housing Retailing/business Public buildings & facilities Highway improvements	High Productive uses with some economic value

Agriculture
  cultivation
  productive grazing
  marginal grazing
  allotments
Forestry
  economic
  marginal
Recreation (intensive)
  sport
  picnic sites
  caravan & camp sites
  car parks
  waterscapes
Recreation (extensive)
  casual/public open space
  country parks
Wildlife
  casual/education
  nature conservation/
  education
	Amenity uses with little or no economic benefit
	
	Low

10 Quarrying

Key ideas
- Quarrying produces many essential materials for human activity.
- Quarrying has a major impact on the landscape and on people living nearby.

10.1 gives information about many of the materials used in the building of brick or stone houses. All of these materials are obtained from quarries. Large amounts are needed: a typical three-bedroomed house in the UK requires 50 tonnes of sand and gravel. These materials are heavy and bulky, so are usually extracted as near as possible to the place of use, to minimise transport costs. Quarrying can have a number of bad effects, on the landscape and on local people's lives (10.2 and 10.3), but its products are invaluable. In addition, quarries provide employment, directly and often also in a related manufacturing plant found alongside or within the quarry.

In the past, quarrying often severely damaged the local environment, and quarry sites were simply abandoned after being worked out, and left derelict. Today UK quarrying operations are much more tightly controlled. Even while quarries are still active, environmental problems can be limited by careful screening of machinery and landscape scars by grassy banks and trees. After the quarry is worked out, the site must by law be properly restored and not left derelict. The 'hole in the ground' left after quarrying can be of very definite value.

- It may be used as a **landfill** site where rubbish of varying kinds is dumped (see Unit 11). (Great care must be taken not to dump poisonous industrial waste in quarries with a high water table where the poison may find its way into ground water drinking supplies.)
- It may be suitable for development as a leisure area (amenity park, lake, etc.)
- It is possible to return some quarries to agricultural use provided the original soil cover is carefully stored before quarrying begins.

Many developing countries have valuable reserves of ores such as iron, copper and aluminium. They can extract these materials by quarrying, sell them to developed countries for cash, and use the money to help their own development. The impact of these quarries on the environment is enormous, and little attempt is made to screen the operation or to reclaim the area after use.

As world supplies of many ores become scarce, quarries are being opened in increasingly remoter areas of both developing and developed countries. For example, much of the iron ore used in Britain now comes from remote areas of Canada and Australia.

Why do you think tackling the environmental problems of quarrying are given a high priority in the UK but a low priority in most developing countries and in some remote areas of developed countries?

▼ 10.1 Materials often used in the building of houses

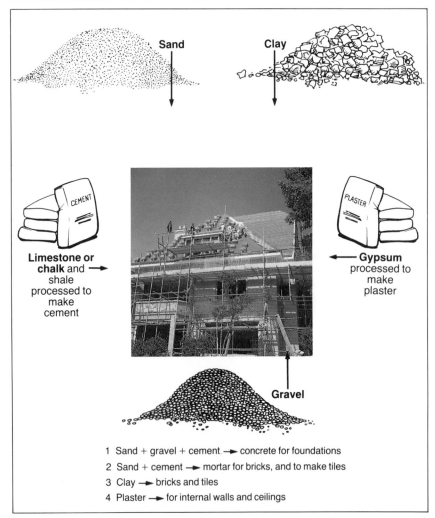

1. Sand + gravel + cement → concrete for foundations
2. Sand + cement → mortar for bricks, and to make tiles
3. Clay → bricks and tiles
4. Plaster → for internal walls and ceilings

▼ 10.2 Limestone quarry

▼ 10.3 Some bad effects of quarrying

Noise: Machinery and blasting in hard rocks
Visual pollution: A scar on the landscape from quarrying and waste generated
Dust: A major problem in chalk and limestone quarrying
Lorries: moving through settlements near quarry
Loss of land: for agriculture, either permanently or temporarily

From Quarry to National Water Sports Centre

The National Water Sports Centre at Holme Pierrepont beside the River Trent near Nottingham (10.4) has facilities specially designed to meet the national needs for rowing, canoeing and water ski-ing. The centre is set in a large 109 hectare country park, which also includes a conference centre and accommodation. The country park remains open throughout the year for more gentle forms of recreation such as walking and angling. In addition there is a horse riding trail around its shores.

▼ 10.5a Holme Pierrepont in 1967

▼ 10.5b Holme Pierrepont National Water Sports Centre, 1981

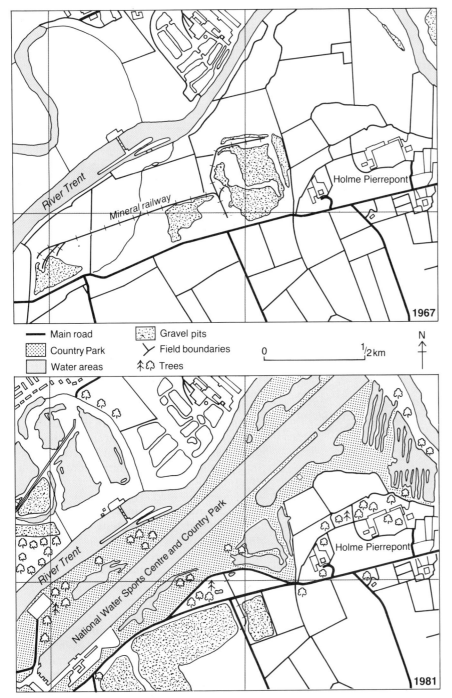

▲ 10.4 National Water Sports Centre at Holme Pierrepont near Nottingham

10.5a is a map of what the area was like in 1967; notice that gravel pits linked together by a mineral railway line occupied much of the area between Holme Pierrepont village and the River Trent. Areas close to the River Trent contain many deposits of sand and gravel which are vital to the local economies but, once the material is removed, large water-filled holes remain. Often these are restored to become recreational attractions for nearby cities but in this case a very imaginative scheme was set up to act as a national centre. 10.5b shows what the area was like in the early 1980s. Notice that a 2000-metre long lake runs through the area of the old gravel workings and that a major new area for extraction has been developed to the south of the centre.

Look carefully again at 10.4 which is a recent photograph of the area. Make a list of developments that have taken place at the National Water Sports Centre since map 10.5b was drawn. To what use do you think the area to the south of the centre should be put when all the sand and gravel have been extracted?

Quarrying 47

11 Rubbish?

Key ideas
- Many different kinds of rubbish result from human activities.
- Traditional methods of rubbish disposal are being increasingly questioned as the benefits of recycling are realised.

Rubbish is produced in homes, factories and offices; in fact wherever we live, work and play. 11.1 shows how the contents of an average dustbin in the UK are made up. Every household in the country produces about 1 tonne of rubbish a year which includes:

- about six trees' worth of paper;
- 50 kg of metal;
- 40 kg of plastic.

Large amounts of this rubbish consist of various forms of packaging, much of which is quite unnecessary. In Britain about 20 million paper bags are thrown away each day.

The collection of domestic rubbish (i.e. from people's homes) must be carefully organised to prevent health hazards. Certain types of industrial rubbish need special handling and are collected separately. These include chemical, asbestos and radioactive waste (see page 69 for details of radioactive waste).

▼ 11.1 The contents of an average UK dustbin

▼ 11.2 Traditional alternatives for waste disposal

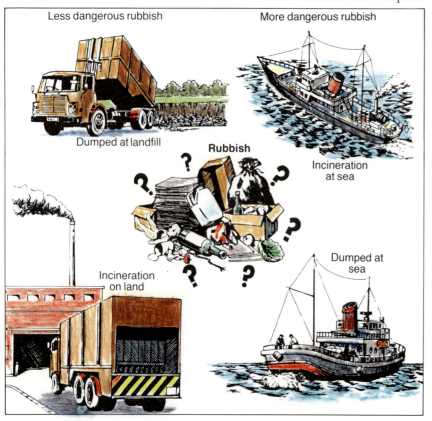

Disposal of waste

Finding somewhere to put the ever-increasing amounts of rubbish is becoming more and more difficult and expensive. In the UK it costs over £750 million a year to dispose of rubbish. 11.2 shows the traditional methods of disposal. Most waste is dumped at **landfills** (see page 50): large holes in the ground which are filled with rubbish, then eventually covered with soil. As the supply of suitable landfill sites runs out, **incineration** is becoming more common. Some particularly dangerous wastes are dumped at sea, or even burned in special incinerator ships. Britain is one of the few countries still burning dangerous chemical waste at sea.

All the traditional methods of rubbish disposal cause problems such as:

- the risk of liquids seeping through landfill sites into ground water supplies;
- air pollution from incinerators, particularly poisonous gas from some plastics and dangerous gases from burning chemical waste on incinerator ships;
- pollution of the sea from dumping waste.

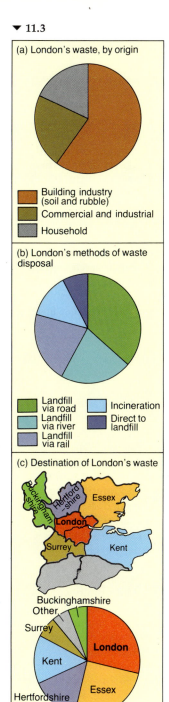

▼ 11.3

(a) London's waste, by origin
- Building industry (soil and rubble)
- Commercial and industrial
- Household

(b) London's methods of waste disposal
- Landfill via road
- Landfill via river
- Landfill via rail
- Incineration
- Direct to landfill

(c) Destination of London's waste

▼ 11.5 Incineration

London's waste

London is the UK's greatest producer of waste. 11.3a shows the proportion of waste from each type of origin; notice that over half is soil and rubble, mainly by-products of the building industry. 11.3b shows how London disposes of its waste. Much of the rubbish is first taken to one of 25 waste-transfer stations where the material is compacted before being transferred by road, rail or river to landfill sites (11.4). At the waste-transfer station in Newham 200 refuse collection lorries are emptied each day but only 45 bulk container lorries are needed to remove the compacted material. The compaction process is necessary because there is a shortage of landfill sites close to London and much rubbish is moved distances of up to 50 km for disposal outside the city (11.3c).

▼ 11.4 Landfill site

▼ 11.6 Recycling potential of dustbin rubbish

Glass	Excellent: large savings of energy
Paper	Excellent: large savings of raw materials
Metal	Good: after sorting
Organic matter	Excellent: easily composted
Plastic	Very limited
Other	Poor: much sorting needed.

Common landfill sites are disused gravel workings in the Thames valley, and quarries in the surrounding area where materials such as clay and chalk are obtained. The compacting station at Hendon, for example, sends 800 tonnes of rubbish per day by rail to a London Brick Company quarry in Bedfordshire. But the number of suitable landfill sites around London is falling because:

- the amount of rubbish being produced is rising and landfill sites are used up;
- the rate of sand and gravel extraction is falling, resulting in fewer new 'holes'.

It is expected that by 1995 over half of London's rubbish will have to be carried more than 65 km to find a suitable 'hole in the ground'.

About 12% of London's rubbish (400 000 tonnes per year) is incinerated (11.5) and London has an advantage in that the heat produced yields electricity worth about £4 million per year. Many towns outside London have incinerators but only a few generate energy. Incinerators are often criticised because of the air pollution they cause, and much research is currently taking place to make them more environmentally friendly.

Too Valuable to Waste

Traditional methods of dealing with rubbish are being increasingly questioned as it has been realised that about 75% of waste products can be re-used or **recycled**. Recycling does not just mean using something again for the same purpose (e.g. returning milk bottles to a dairy for refill) but also includes a whole range of resource recovery activities such as industrial recycling of paper and glass (see pages 52–3) and incineration of certain kinds of rubbish to produce energy. 11.6 gives details of the recycling potential of the various dustbin contents in 11.1. The main reasons for recycling are:

- to conserve natural resources and reduce environmental damage from extractive industries;
- to ease the pressure for new landfill (waste-disposal) sites;
- to reduce waste-disposal costs;
- to save energy;
- possibly to reduce the need to import raw materials.

There is increasing public concern over conservation of resources and prevention of pollution. Recycling of rubbish is a very simple and practical way in which individual people can show that they care about the environment.

Rubbish? 49

▼ 11.7 Advantages and disadvantages of landfill

Advantages
1. Usually the cheapest method of rubbish disposal.
2. Sites are usually out of sight and rubbish is quickly disposed of.
3. Can be used to produce landfill gas for energy.
4. Once tip is full it can be used for productive farming.

Disadvantages
1. Can be unsightly, smelly, and attract vermin.
2. Increase in traffic on roads to site.
3. Water passing through tip can pollute ground water.
4. Landfill gas can be dangerous.
5. Settling continues for many years after tip is full: land cannot be used for building.
6. Waste of valuable resources which could be recycled.

▼ 11.8 Cell tipping: collecting gas produced from decomposed rubbish

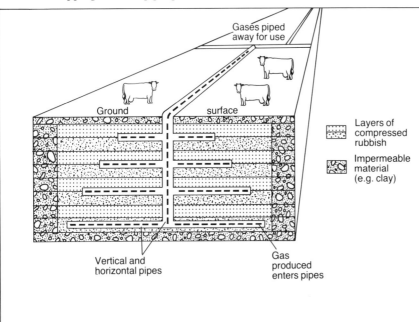

▼ 11.9 Landfill gas sites in the USA

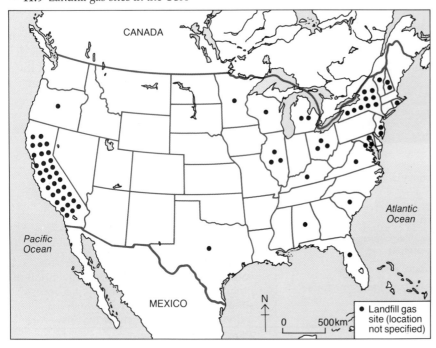

Landfill

Most of the UK's rubbish is sent to one of the 4000 landfill sites. Much of the rubbish could be recycled (see pages 52–53) but landfill will remain the major disposal method until well into the next century. The advantages and disadvantages of landfill are compared in 11.7. In March 1986, at the village of Loscoe in Derbyshire, rubbish in an old brickworks pit had generated landfill gas which ignited in a nearby bungalow injuring several people and damaging property. This incident and others like it illustrate the possible hazards associated with landfill. However it is increasingly being realised that the gas could be used to advantage as a rich source of energy. In order to tap this energy source, the design of a landfill site must be carefully controlled.

Landfill gas

The modern landfill site acts as a 'bio-reactor' in which bacteria in the waste cause complicated decomposition reactions that produce methane and carbon dioxide gases. Landfill gas in the UK could produce energy equivalent to around 1.5 million tonnes of coal per year in 1990 and around 3.0 million tonnes of coal by the year 2000. To collect the gas a technique called cell tipping must be used (11.8). An area of 1–6 hectares is chosen which has impermeable (gas and water tight) floor and walls. The rubbish is compacted as it is tipped and, when the cell is full, it is sealed to prevent rain water entering. The sealing and compaction of the rubbish greatly reduce the amount of oxygen in the cell and create conditions ideal for landfill gas production. The gas begins to be produced within 6 months, peaks after about 2 years and continues for 15–20 years at a reducing rate. While the gas is being collected the surface of the cell can be used for pasture. After cleansing to remove impurities, landfill gas can be used in a number of ways:

- as a fuel for boilers in factories adjacent to the landfill site;
- to generate electricity;
- to replace natural gas;
- (after being liquified) as a fuel for vehicles.

In the USA there are some 70 landfill gas sites (11.9) mainly being used to generate electricity. In Europe, West Germany and the UK are at the forefront of landfill gas development. One UK development is looking at the possibility of adding sewage sludge to landfill material to increase gas output.

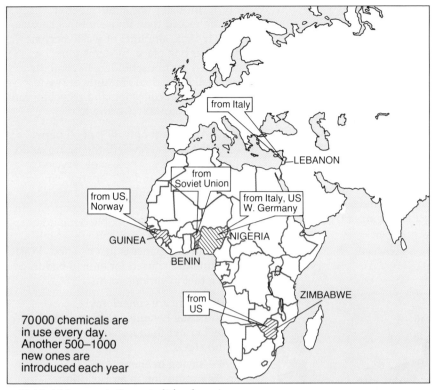

▲ 11.10 Africa: waste 'imported' for dumping

70000 chemicals are in use every day. Another 500–1000 new ones are introduced each year

Toxic waste: a growing problem

The problem of disposing of chemical waste is growing. Pressure from environmental and health groups has led to increased use of incineration (on land and at sea), recycling and safer landfill sites, but has not persuaded industrial companies to produce less toxic waste. Some companies are dumping more at sea, and waters are becoming dangerously polluted. Certain countries have quite strict regulations prohibiting the dumping of toxic waste and these countries often try to dump their waste in other countries where regulations are more lax or nonexistent. Developing countries are particularly vulnerable and some have been exploited by companies from the developed world offering cash in exchange for dumping sites. Africa is probably worst affected (11.10); for example, one Italian–Nigerian company dumped 17 600 drums of dangerous chemicals in an uncontrolled landfill site in Nigeria.

The information in 11.11 is about an incident which took place in August 1989. *What do you think should be done to improve the disposal of chemical waste?*

▼ 11.11 *Today*, 17 August 1989

We will send no more toxic waste pledge Canadians

by SIMON CORBETT

PROTESTERS have won a battle to stop deadly chemical waste being imported from Canada.

The Canadian Government halted further shipments after dockers refused to unload 100 tonnes of toxic PCBs at Liverpool yesterday.

Earlier in the week, another ship was refused permission to unload a similar cargo at Tilbury and was sent back across the Atlantic.

Now Canada has scrapped plans to send 13 more loads to a reprocessing plant at Pontypool in South Wales.

The Russian-built Nedezhad Obukhaba was allowed to unload the rest of its cargo before being ordered to sail out of Liverpool.

Delighted protesters praised the dockers' action.

Crisis

"We were told by the Government months ago that none of this material would ever arrive in Britain," said spokesman David Powell.

"Now look what has happened. The rest of the world is using Britain as a dumping ground.

"The dockers gave us a great reception and their message was not to worry. They will make sure this waste won't get through Liverpool."

Greenpeace toxic waste campaigner Tim Birch said: "By allowing the importation of toxic waste into this country, the UK government is encouraging the global toxic waste crisis.

"The only environmentally safe solution is a reduction of toxic waste at source."

He said government policy on toxic waste was "making a mockery" of its new Green image, adding: "They are simply putting profit before the protection of the environment."

Liverpool Labour MP Terry Field said the arrival of the Russian ship in the city was "a scandal and a crime."

Environment Secretary Chris Patten said there was "no reason whatsoever" to fear the cargo on environmental grounds.

He said there were tough regulations governing the import of waste and dismissed allegations that Britain was open to any imports.

"If waste has come into this country in a way which breaks our regulations it must go back where it came from," he said.

"The fact is, we haven't been and we are not going to be the dustbin for the world."

11.13a Bottle bank

11.13b Paper collection 'igloo'

11.13c Can collection

Recycling Begins at Home

The idea of recycling waste is not new (11.12). However there is a growing sense of urgency to organise recycling properly as we realise that our wasteful way of life is squandering the earth's resources and threatening the planet with pollution. 11.13 shows the collection of three common substances (glass, paper and aluminium) that are increasingly being recycled. If this recycling is to be successful, as many people as possible must take part and see recycling as the norm and not as a temporary concern. Industry has a much better recycling record than householders because relatively large amounts of waste become available at one place. Systems must be established for householders to combine their small individual amounts of waste together so that collection and recycling can become economically worthwhile.

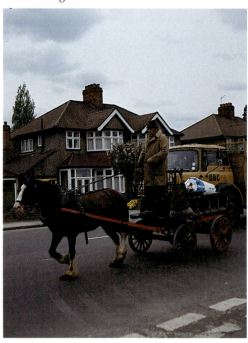

11.12 'Rag and bone' merchant

Paper At present only 30% of all paper used in the UK is recycled: the figure could potentially be 85%. The use of recycled paper saves trees and also energy, since its manufacture uses only half the amount of energy and water used to make paper from trees. Currently, most people demand crisp, bright, white paper even though a high-quality recycled paper is just as good. Waste paper can also be used for animal bedding and as a fuel in various forms.

Metals There are considerable environmental benefits in using scrap iron and steel rather than iron ore to make new iron and steel.

- a 74% saving in energy,
- an 86% reduction in air pollution,
- a 40% reduction in water use.

Food and drink cans can also be recycled *if* they can be collected in sufficient quantities. Aluminium cans are the most expensive to produce as it takes 31 barrels of oil to make 1 tonne of aluminium from imported bauxite ore compared with only 2 barrels of oil when aluminium scrap is used. In the UK, 1500 million drinks cans made entirely from aluminium are bought each year: clearly the recycling potential is enormous.

Plastics Over 30% of plastics in the UK are used in packaging. Some can be re-used, but most are simply thrown away. Most plastics are produced from oil and use up lots of energy. Many plastics cannot be recycled, including the large clear plastic bottles with moulded bases used by the soft drinks industry. They can, however, be re-used. For example, the Coca Cola company has introduced a bottle deposit system (returnable) in several US states and in West Germany. Personal re-use of plastic cartons, carrier bags, etc. is another way of cutting down waste.

Incineration of dustbin and other rubbish is also a form of recycling as the energy produced by the burning rubbish can be re-used. (However, burning plastic can produce poisonous gas.) 11.14 gives details of how much household waste is recycled to create energy in various European countries.

Britain lags behind many other developed countries in the field of recycling.

What do you think (i) individuals (ii) the government (iii) companies should do to improve the situation?

11.14 Dustbin energy league

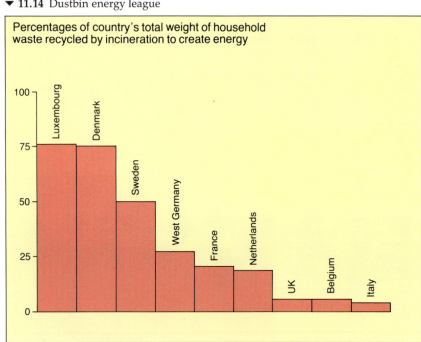

Carry out a class survey to see how much of their rubbish each family recycles and discuss ways of increasing the amount.

What recycling schemes (if any) does your school take part in? Suggest ways in which more could be done and suggest how any money raised could be used.

Glass 11.15 shows how glass is recycled. The container industry uses 66% of all glass but only about 30% of the raw material used is **cullet** (broken recycled glass). The main reasons for recycling glass are

- it saves energy,
- it reduces the number of quarries needed for sand and limestone,
- it saves money in terms of raw materials and by reducing the cost of rubbish disposal.

Glass bottles and jars can also be returned for refilling. Such a system is used with milk bottles which have an average lifespan of 25 return journeys.

Some people think that bottles and jars should be of a standard size and shape to help re-use but the container manufacturers are not in favour of this as it would obviously reduce the need for their product.

Because the quarried raw materials for glass making are not in short supply the main reason for recycling glass is to save energy. Bottle re-use schemes would save much more energy but they have not been successful and so bottle banks remain the preferable alternative to throwing bottles in the dustbin. Bottle banks have also had the very desirable effect of making people aware that recycling is an important issue which affects every individual in society.

▼ 11.15 Recycling glass

Sort your saved empty bottles into returnable and recyclable.

Put bottles and jars in the correct colour compartment: green, brown or clear.

Full bottle banks are emptied at a central depot. Large loads are then delivered to glass recycling centre.

Glass bottles and jars are crushed into small pieces (called cullet); paper, plastic and metal are removed.

Cullet is mixed with soda ash, sand and limestone and heated to 1500 °C in special furnaces. Pieces of molten glass drop into moulds and are blown into bottles or jars.

Recycled bottles and jars are checked and taken to food and drink manufacturers to be filled. When empty it is hoped the recycling process starts again.

12 Energy

Key ideas
- The availability of energy resources plays a vital role in the lives of individual people and the development of countries.
- World patterns of energy production and consumption are very uneven.
- Electricity production is increasing rapidly, causing concern for the environment.

Since the early 1970s, energy consumption has been increasing more rapidly than ever before. 12.1 shows that **fossil fuels**, such as crude oil, natural gas and coal, are still our main sources of energy. These are also sometimes called **non-renewable** fuels because, once the world's supplies have been used up, it will be impossible to obtain any more. Hydro-electric power (HEP) is an example of a **renewable** energy source, because it is generated by water, which will not run out. 12.1 shows the **primary sources of energy**. Much of our power supply comes in the form of electricity which is generated from these primary sources.

12.1 only shows those energy sources which are traded or sold. This gives a very accurate view of energy use in the developed world, but is less helpful in understanding the position in the developing world. Although the situation varies enormously from country to country, about one-half to three-quarters of the energy used in developing countries comes from **biomass fuels**. These include all organic fuels, with timber making up about 85% (12.2), animal manure 13% and small amounts of household and plant waste. Animal energy (12.3) is still important, particularly in rural areas where energy sources such as oil or coal are scarce, and where finance and/or expertise to exploit other sources are lacking.

A number of less conventional energy sources are being developed in various countries, but at present none provides a major source of power.

- **Geothermal energy** comes from naturally occurring heat within rock formations below the earth's surface.
- **Ocean power** includes
  (i) tidal power, where the rise and fall of tides is used to turn giant turbines;
  (ii) wave power, which involves capturing the energy of the waves in floating generators;
  (iii) ocean thermal energy conversion, whereby temperature differences between warm surface water and cool deep water are used;
  (iv) ocean currents tapped by anchoring turbines to the sea bed;
  (v) salinity gradient energy, gained by mixing fresh and salt water.
- **Passive solar energy systems** rely on walls, windows and other structures to provide heat and cooling.
- **Active solar energy systems** (such as solar panels) collect and use the energy of the sun to generate electric power.
- **Wind energy** uses the power of the wind, either in windmills or wind generators.

▼ 12.1 World energy consumption

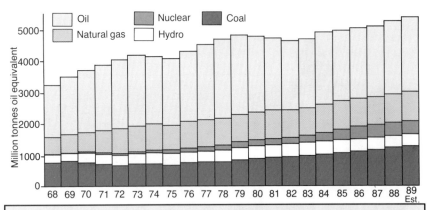

▼ 12.2 Wood being used as a fuel in Mali

▼ 12.3 Animal power in China

Oil: rose steadily from 1968 to a peak of 3124 million tonnes in 1979. Consumption then fell until the mid 1980s. 1986 and 1987 saw a small increase of just over 10%.

Natural gas: consumption has steadily increased from just over 700 million tonnes in 1968 to 1556 million tonnes in 1987. At present increasing by about 4% per year.

Nuclear: has grown rapidly to over 400 million tonnes in 1987. Increasing by about 6% to 8% per year.

HEP: has grown steadily since 1968, from 373 million tonnes to 524 million tonnes. The present rate of growth is between 1% and 2% per year.

Coal: remained fairly stable from 1968 to 1978, but since that time has grown steadily from 1860 million tonnes (1978) to 2386 million tonnes (1987). Now increasing by about 2% to 3% per year.

Describe the changes in the total world energy consumption for this period.

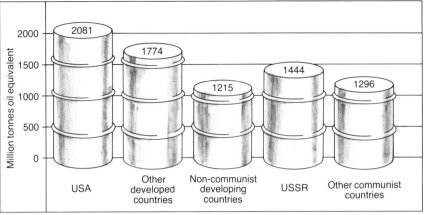

▲ 12.4a Total consumption of energy, 1988

▼ 12.4b Per capita consumption of energy,

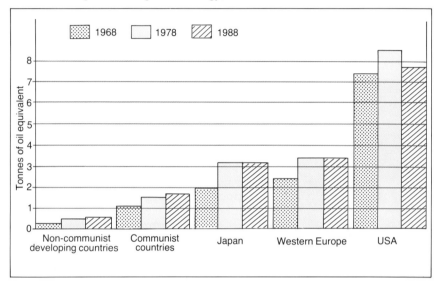

▼ 12.5 Regional energy consumption patterns, 1988

▼ 12.6 Fossil fuel reserves: how long will they last?

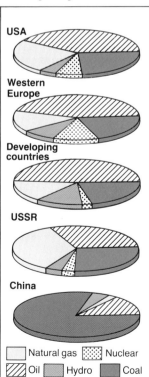

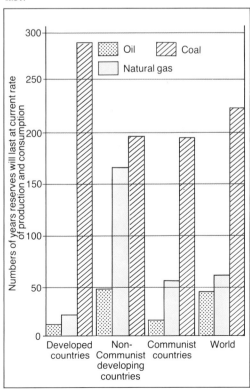

Fair Shares?

The rate of energy consumption varies enormously in different parts of the world. 12.4a shows that the USA uses not only more energy than any other country, but more than all other developed countries put together. This means that a country with less than 5% of the world's population uses almost 27% of the world's energy.

12.4b shows the average amount of energy consumed by each person in different parts of the world, and how consumption has changed. Notice that consumption in the USA is well over twice that of the other developed region shown: Western Europe. In fact, the average American consumed over 35 times as much energy as a person from a non-communist developing country in 1968 and 15 times more in 1988, even though US consumption fell in the 1980s.

12.4b also shows that consumption in developed countries is levelling out. This contrasts with the developing and communist countries where consumption is still rising quite rapidly.

Regional patterns

The type of energy used varies enormously around the world (12.5). The USA, Western Europe and the developing countries depend heavily on oil. As they have relatively small reserves (12.6) much has to be bought from other countries. This means that far more oil enters into world trade than any other energy type.

12.5 also shows that China relies heavily on its own supplies of coal; similarly the USSR has plentiful supplies of natural gas, in addition to oil and coal. It is also noticeable that nuclear power is far more important in developed countries.

12.6 shows how long the world's reserves of the three major fossil fuels will last at the present rates of consumption and production. It must of course be remembered that it is likely that more supplies will be found, and that production rates may rise or fall. It is clear that coal is likely to last far longer than oil and natural gas. It can also be noticed that developed countries have only just over 10 years' supply of oil and 20 years' supply of natural gas left. As supplies diminish, prices will rise for everyone.

Use the diagrams on this page to describe how the following vary from country to country:
(a) per capita energy consumption,
(b) the use of different energy sources.
Why might the estimates made in 12.6 be proved incorrect?

Energy 55

Electricity Generation

Electricity is a **secondary energy source**, because another energy source is needed to make it. It has the great advantage of being suited to very rapid transportation over great distances, using transmission lines. It is also a very flexible form of energy. (Think how many pieces of equipment you use each day which rely upon electricity.)

The raw materials used to make electricity vary from country to country, according to the energy resources that are available. At the present time in England and Wales about 50% of the power stations are coal-fired, 17% use gas turbines, 12% are nuclear, and a small number use oil, a mixture of oil and coal, or pumped storage (water). There are also seven small hydro-electric power stations.

12.7 shows the Drax station, which is situated between Selby and Goole in North Yorkshire. It is one of Western Europe's largest coal-fired power stations with a total output of 4000 megawatts. At full power, it consumes 37 000 tonnes of coal every day, delivered in train loads of over 1000 tonnes from the nearby North Yorkshire coalfield. A **'merry-go-round'** system is used, in which the trains run round in a circle, and are unloaded without stopping, before returning to the colliery to collect more coal. The station is situated on the south bank of the River Ouse, so the river supplies all the water that is needed for cooling. The huge quantities of ash produced when coal is burned can cause problems, but at Drax a vacant site was available next to the station, at Barlow, where the ash could be disposed of. The site is also near to the M18 and M62, allowing rapid movement of materials that must come by road.

12.8 shows how a coal-fired power station works. The process of generating and transmitting electricity produces a number of environmental problems. Burning coal produces sulphur dioxide and oxides of nitrogen, and these gases are sent high into the atmosphere from the boiler chimney, causing acid rain (see Unit 18). Once electricity has been produced, it is distributed along electric transmission lines. These give off **electromagnetic radiation**, and there is increasing concern that this has a number of harmful effects on people nearby, from headaches and loss of concentration, to cancer and heart attacks. In 1986, a Houston (USA) power company was ordered to pay $25 million in damages for erecting a power line within 60 metres of three schools. It has now had to move these power lines. Some people also feel that power stations and transmission lines cause a great deal of visual pollution.

Using the information on this page and an atlas, draw a labelled sketch map to show the location of the Drax power station. Describe the main advantages of its site and situation.

▼ 12.7 Drax power station

▼ 12.8 How a coal-fired power station works

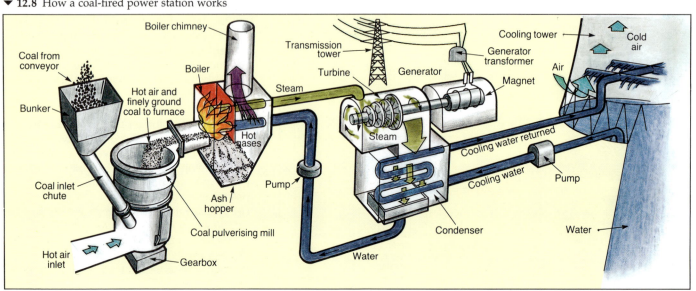

56 Energy

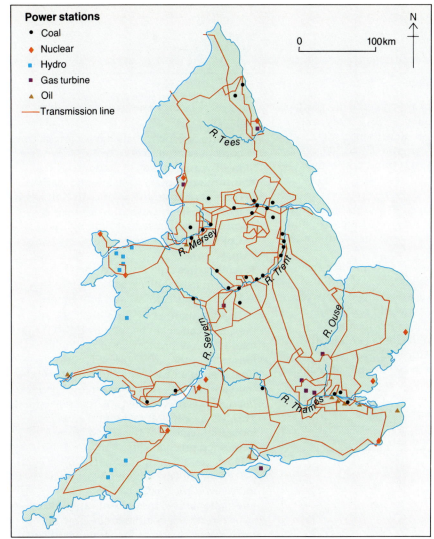

▲ 12.9 Location of power stations, England and Wales (Scotland has its own electricity network)

Describe and explain the pattern of location of each of the different types of power station shown on 12.9.

Suggest reasons for the seasonal and daily differences in demand shown in 12.10.

▼ 12.10 Demand for electricity, England and Wales

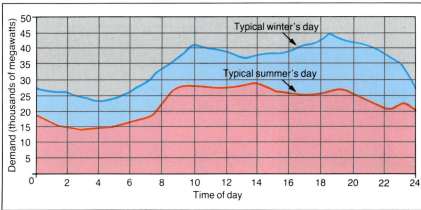

Power Stations

12.9 shows the location of the power stations and supergrid system of electric transmission lines in England and Wales.

- Coal-fired power stations are mostly found on or near coalfields to minimise transport costs. Within the coalfields, locations on large rivers (e.g. Trent) are particularly favoured, because water is available for steam generation and cooling. Power stations are also found at ports (e.g. London) where cheap transport of coal by ship is possible; or in areas of particularly high demand (e.g. Didcot on the Upper Thames) even if these are quite far away from coalfields.
- Nuclear power stations were first built at remote locations (e.g. Dungeness in Kent) because of fears of radiation leaks. More recent ones have been built closer to populated centres. Coastal sites are favoured because of the need for water in steam-making and cooling. Areas with firm bedrock to support the reactors are essential.
- Hydro-electric power stations are usually found in upland areas (such as North Wales), where there is heavy rainfall and deep valleys which can be used to create reservoirs. They are therefore remote from the main centres of population.
- Gas turbine power stations are distributed throughout the country, to meet short-term demand for power.
- Oil-fired stations are found near oil refineries, on coasts with deep harbours that can take large oil-tankers. Sometimes this means that they are rather remote (e.g. Pembroke), but some are situated near to large cities (e.g. London and Southampton).

All of these power stations are connected to the **National Grid** network of transmission lines. This means that energy can be moved fairly readily from one area to another. At times of high demand, electricity may also be transferred from Scotland, and from France (via undersea cables).

The daily plan for generating power is based upon forecasts of the demand. Enough power must be available to meet unexpected demand, but producing too much wastes money as electricity cannot be stored. 12.10 shows that power demands vary through the day and throughout the year. Cold winter days mean a particularly high general demand, while the end of a very popular television programme can mean a sudden short-term increase in demand as millions of viewers turn on their electric kettles.

To meet basic demand, low-cost **base load** stations (mostly coal-fired, some nuclear) operate continuously. Higher-cost stations are brought into use as demand rises. The Ffestiniog pumped storage plant is particularly helpful in meeting rapid increases in demand, as it is capable of moving to full power in a matter of minutes. The gas turbine stations are used in a similar way to make up the power required at peak periods.

Energy 57

13 Coal

Key ideas
- Reserves of coal are more evenly spread in the world and will last much longer than other types of fossil fuels.
- Mining coal can bring wealth to an area but can cause a number of environmental problems.

On a world map, locate and name the countries listed in 13.3. Colour exporting countries in red and importing countries in green. What does the pattern shown suggest about the likely trade routes for coal?

Reserves of coal are more evenly distributed than those of oil and gas (13.1). They will also last much longer: at present consumption rates, around 250 to 300 years. However, the USA, the USSR and China have by far the largest reserves. With the exception of China, the largest reserves are also in more developed countries. Asia and Latin America have relatively little coal, and almost 90% of Africa's reserves are in South Africa.

Reserves are constantly changing as coal is used, more coal is discovered, and new mining techniques are developed. Between 1981 and 1987, known world reserves increased by 16%. This growth was particularly marked in China (49.3%), the USA (28.2%) and Africa (22.5%).

There are hundreds of varieties of coal, but generally they are divided into three major types.
- **Lignite** or brown coals have a low carbon content of around 60% to 70%. They are mostly used in power stations.
- **Bituminous coals** have a higher carbon content of around 80% and give off more light and heat. **Gascoal** has a high gas content and is used for making gas. **Coking coal**, another variety, is used to make coke.
- **Anthracites** are very hard coals which have at least 90% carbon content. They burn with great heat and little smoke.

The dominance of China, the USA and the USSR can again be seen in 13.2. Of the total 1988 coal production of 2247 million tonnes, less than 20% entered world trade. Coal is such a heavy and bulky material that transporting it is very expensive. Whenever possible it is used close to where it is mined. This has meant that many of the major industrial regions of the world have developed on coalfields.

However, even this relatively low percentage of coal entering world trade is an increase on the past. Over 75% of international coal movements are now by sea, since the development of large bulk carriers has greatly reduced transport costs. As a result there has been a steady rise in the amount of coal traded over very large distances.

Japan (which has very small reserves) is by far the major importer (13.3). It needs coking coal for its iron and steel industry and bituminous coal for its power stations. Australia is the leading exporter, with almost half of its total production being sent to Japan.

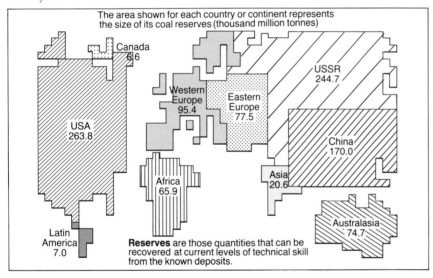

▼ 13.1 World coal reserves, 1988

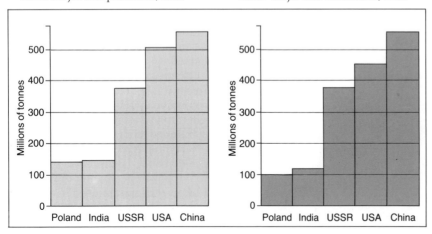

▼ 13.2a Major coal producers, 1988

▼ 13.2b Major coal consumers, 1988

▼ 13.3 Coal trade, 1988 (million tonnes)

Exports		Imports	
Australia	92	Japan	89
USA	76	S. Korea	21
S. Africa	46	Italy	20
Poland	34	France	17
Canada	26	Canada	13
USSR	25	Netherlands	12
China	10	Taiwan	11
W. Germany	8	UK	11

▲ 13.4 A coal seam

▼ 13.5 Opencast coal mining

Mining Techniques

Coal is found in layers called **seams** (13.4), which vary in width from a few millimetres to several metres. The rocks in which seams of coal are found are called **coal measures**. Mining is usually carried out using one of three methods.

- **Adit** or **drift mining** is used to obtain coal from horizontal or gently sloping seams that **outcrop** (come to the surface) on sloping ground. These are usually relatively small mines, and many have been worked out.
- **Shaft mining** is used when coal lies hundreds of metres below the surface. Vertical shafts are sunk down to the level of the seams. Horizontal, or gently sloping tunnels are then dug out to obtain the coal. This is the most expensive and dangerous type of mining. Many smaller mines where seams are thin, or where modern machines cannot be used, have been closed down, even before all of the coal has been removed, because production costs were too high. Within Britain, there is an increasing concentration on a few very large modern mines, where seams are thick and mechanisation is easy. Once a shaft mine has been worked out it is abandoned and, until reclamation takes place, derelict buildings and ugly spoil heaps can ruin the landscape. In some areas the soil and rock above the coal seam sink down into the gap left by the coal that has been removed **(subsidence)**. This may damage any structures built on the surface.
- **Opencast mining** is used when the coal seams lie relatively near to the surface, usually less than 100 metres. The rock layers on top of the coal, known as **overburden**, are removed, and coal is dug out by mechanical diggers. This is a much cheaper and safer method than shaft mining. Huge areas can be laid waste by this method, and in many countries planning regulations now ensure that the land is returned to its former condition.

Much of the recent growth in world coal output results from new large opencast mining operations. Often these exploit lower-quality coals, and 95% of the world's lignite is now mined in this way. The size of individual opencast mines has increased: a single mine can produce 20 million tonnes a year. The development of large machines (13.5) has also speeded up extraction considerably.

China

China is the world's largest coal producer, with estimated deposits of 800 billion tonnes of coal, of which around 170 billion are recoverable at the present time. Unlike most other countries, where there has been an increasing concentration on a small number of modern mines, much of the production in China comes from a large number of small mines (13.6). A decision was taken by the government in 1983 to allow individuals and small groups to mine coal, after which some 61 000 new pits were opened.

There are also a few large more modern pits, concerned mainly with producing coal for export. (Coal sales are seen as one way of speeding up China's development plans.) One such mine is the Antaibao Number 1 Mine at Pingshuo near Datong in Shanxi province (13.7), which began production in 1987. This vast opencast mine will eventually produce 15 million tonnes of coal a year. The existing railway links between Datong and the port of Qinhuangdao on the Bohai Sea are being improved, including the construction of a new line just for coal traffic. Another 30 small pits will also use this line which will eventually be able to take 100 million tonnes of coal a year for export from Qinhuangdao (13.7).

Railway construction is also taking place to improve links between the mines in the southern part of Shanxi province and the port of Shijiu. This large port will then become a major coal-exporting centre.

Shanxi province as a whole produces approximately 25% of China's coal, and about 50% of its exports. By the year 2000 it is estimated that this province alone will produce 400 million tonnes of coal a year.

▼ 13.7 Export routes for Shanxi coal

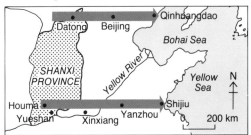

▼ 13.6 Small coal mine, China

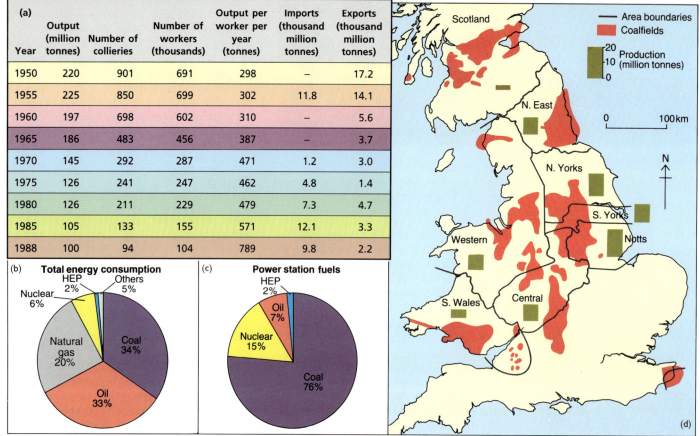

▲ 13.8 Coal in Britain, 1988

(a)

Year	Output (million tonnes)	Number of collieries	Number of workers (thousands)	Output per worker per year (tonnes)	Imports (thousand million tonnes)	Exports (thousand million tonnes)
1950	220	901	691	298	–	17.2
1955	225	850	699	302	11.8	14.1
1960	197	698	602	310	–	5.6
1965	186	483	456	387	–	3.7
1970	145	292	287	471	1.2	3.0
1975	126	241	247	462	4.8	1.4
1980	126	211	229	479	7.3	4.7
1985	105	133	155	571	12.1	3.3
1988	100	94	104	789	9.8	2.2

Describe and give reasons for the changes shown in 13.8a. Describe the pattern of coal production shown in 13.8d.

British Coal

Since the mid 1950s coal production in Britain has been steadily declining (13.8a), and the 1988 total was 44% of the 1955 total. However, coal remains the most important energy source in Britain, followed very closely by oil (13.8b). In terms of power station fuel, coal is still by far the most important (13.8c), its consumption being over five times more than nuclear fuel, its nearest rival.

The main reasons for the decline in coal production are as follows.

- Much of the most easily mined and best-quality coal has already been mined, resulting in the remaining reserves being more costly to mine.
- Since the 1950s alternative energy sources have been developed, or have grown greatly in importance. Imported oil, and North Sea oil and natural gas, have often been cheaper than coal, and are more efficient and cleaner. Nuclear power has become more important.
- A number of formerly important coal users – steamships, steam railway engines and coal-gas works – have almost completely disappeared.
- Most of Britain's exports of coal have been lost to other countries (see page 58) which have much lower production costs. Britain now imports around 10 million tonnes of this cheap foreign coal each year (13.8a).

Although coal production has been falling, the number of collieries (13.8a) and the number of miners show a much more rapid decline. In 1988 the number of collieries was 11% of the 1955 total, and the number of miners 15% of the 1955 total. This is because many of the older smaller pits, which were unsuited to the use of modern machines, have been closed. Production has instead been concentrated on more modern, and often deeper, pits which can easily be mechanised (13.9) and therefore need far fewer workers. The average age of miners has also declined, particularly since 1970. This is largely due to generous redundancy payments given to miners who volunteered to retire, or to find another job, when mines closed. The overall result has been a smaller but more efficient industry, with each miner in 1988 producing over 2½ times as much coal as in 1955.

13.8d shows the coalfields of Britain, but not all of them are being worked at the present time. The total production from each area can also be seen. The Yorkshire/Nottinghamshire and Derbyshire Coalfield is by far the most productive. The output per worker shift in Scotland and South Wales is far below the national average, and mines in these areas are under threat of closure.

▼ 13.9 Range-drum shearer cutting and loading coal

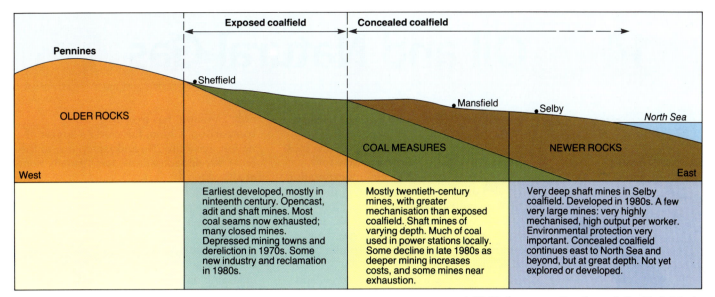

▲ 13.10 A cross-section through the Yorkshire/Nottinghamshire and Derbyshire Coalfield

▼ 13.11 Stilling Fleet Mine

▼ 13.12 Arguments for and against Hawkhurst Moor Colliery

For	Against
1. 'Warwickshire Thick' coal seam up to 7 m thick of high-quality coal. Could be extracted at low cost in a large highly mechanised mine. 2. Coal needed as supplies from older mines decline. 3. Coal needed as oil and natural gas supplies run out. 4. Coal produced would reduce need to import costly fuels in future. 5. Jobs created for 700 people during construction and, when mine opens, for 1800 miners. Many more jobs will be created indirectly in servicing the colliery and its workers. 6. Local firms will benefit from orders for equipment to build mine. 7. Businesses in the area will benefit from about £15 million earned by miners working there each year. 8. The mines will be specially designed and screened with trees, to fit in with the landscape. 9. All land used for tipping will be reclaimed. 10. New road and rail links will reduce environmental impact of movement of coal from the mine. 11. The depth of the mine (1000 m) should mean little subsidence.	1. This is **greenbelt** land. Will further reduce area of countryside between Coventry and Birmingham. 2. Good-quality farmland will be lost, and farm workers will lose jobs. 3. Countryside will be lost, removing habitat for wildlife and leisure opportunities for people. 4. The new road and rail traffic will lead to greater noise and atmospheric pollution. There will also be greater congestion on already crowded roads. 5. The colliery is very close to the urban area of Coventry, and will be an eyesore. 6. It would be much better to spend money on developing other energy sources which do not harm the environment in the way that coal does. 7. Property prices will fall in areas close to the mine and new road and railway. People living nearby will be disturbed. 8. Buildings over the area mined may suffer from subsidence.

The new order

The section through the Yorkshire, Nottinghamshire and Derbyshire Coalfield (13.10) shows a number of the major changes that have taken place since the 1960s. The first mines to be developed were on the **exposed coalfield** in the west, where the coal measures came to the surface. As these mines were exhausted or became increasingly uneconomic to mine, mines were developed in the **concealed coalfield**. Here newer rocks lie over the coal measures, and mines are deeper.

The deepest and most modern mines are in the Selby Coalfield, which has particularly rich seams of coal. The best coal seam, the Barnsley Seam, has been described as 'a 2 metre band of coal the size of the Isle of Wight'. This seam alone contains 600 million tonnes of coal, although only 330 million tonnes will be mined, to reduce the risks of subsidence. The five collieries at Selby Coalfield are among the most modern and highly mechanised in the world, and continually break British and European productivity records. Much has been done to lessen the visual impact of the collieries (13.11), although some local people still feel that they are an eyesore.

Whenever it is planned to open a new mine there is concern that the damage done to the environment and to the quality of people's lives may be too high. 13.12 explores some of the opinions being voiced about the proposed colliery at Hawkhurst Moor near Coventry. *Consider the various arguments, and then describe with reasons whether or not you consider that approval for the colliery should be given.*

14 Oil and Natural Gas

Key ideas
- Crude oil is a vital resource, and its concentration in a few areas results in large quantities being transported around the world each year.
- Sales of crude oil and natural gas can bring economic benefit to an area, but their production and movement can cause environmental problems.

Petroleum is called **crude oil** in its natural state, and is therefore often known simply as oil. It has a wide variety of uses, the most important being as a power source for vehicles, industry and electricity generation. It is also used as a raw material in the chemical industry. Oil is essential for what we think of as a modern way of life and, for countries with small or no reserves, importing what they need can prove very expensive.

14.1 shows the world's oil reserves, and emphasises the dominant position of the Middle East. Saudi Arabia alone has almost 19% of the world's reserves, and the tiny country of Kuwait, with a population of only 2 million, has over 10%. In comparison, China, the world's largest nation, has only 2%, and Japan, one of the most developed nations, has virtually none at all.

Crude oil is a **non-renewable** fossil fuel and, at the present rate of consumption, the proven reserves will last for 41 years. However, these reserves are growing all the time as new exploration takes place in many parts of the world, and the technology for obtaining oil improves. As recently as 1979 there were only 27 years' reserves left! The world's total reserves more than doubled, between 1968 and 1988, but by far the biggest increase was in the Middle East, as 14.2 shows. It is very likely that in the next 25 years the world will become even more dependent upon the Middle East for its crude oil supplies. Also, as the most accessible reserves are used up, new finds are likely to be in more remote locations or at greater depth.

14.3 shows the leading position of the USSR and the USA as oil producers and consumers. The USSR has about 7% of the world's reserves, and is able to export crude oil, particularly to Eastern Europe. On the other hand the USA has less than 4% of the world's reserves, and these are running out rapidly. At the present rate of consumption they will last for less than 10 years. The USA consumes 26% of the total world production of crude oil, and imports 25% of the crude oil that enters world trade. It is likely to remain by far the major importer of oil, particularly dependent upon the Middle East for its supplies in the future.

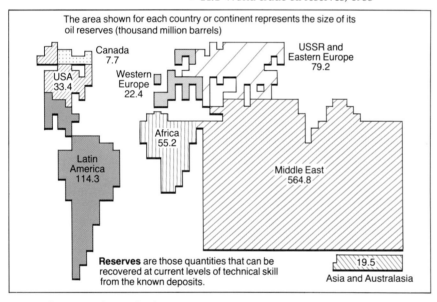

▼ 14.1 World crude oil reserves, 1988

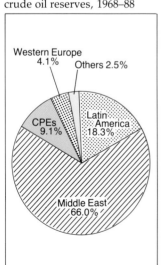

▼ 14.2 Location of growth of crude oil reserves, 1968–88

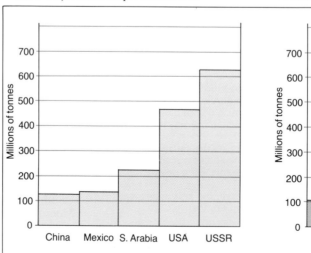

▼ 14.3a Major crude oil producers, 1988

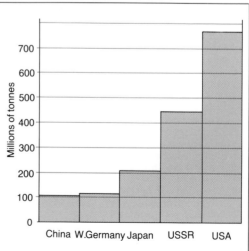

▼ 14.3b Major crude oil consumers, 1988

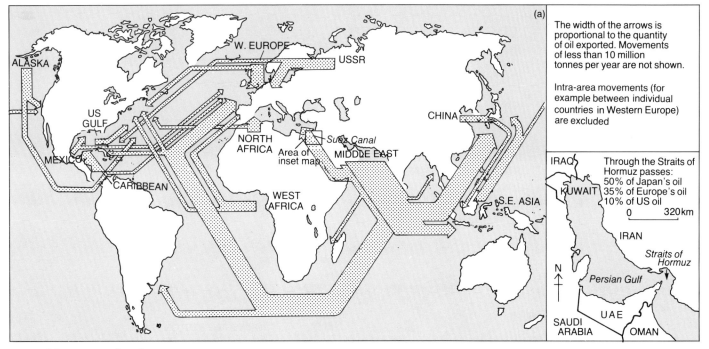

▲ 14.4 Movements of crude oil by sea (It must be remembered that 14.4 does not show movement of crude oil or oil products by pipeline)

What potential trouble spots can you identify on 14.4 that might endanger oil supplies? What could the importing nations do to safeguard their supplies?

Oil Lifelines

The major movements of crude oil by sea are shown in 14.4. The dominance of the Middle East as an exporting area is clear. *Describe the major movements of oil, noting both the exporting and importing areas.*

Certain sea lanes are particularly important for transporting oil and, when wars occur in these areas, supplies can be disrupted. The Persian Gulf is of vital importance, particularly the Straits of Hormuz (14.4b). Vast quantities of oil from Saudi Arabia, Kuwait, the United Arab Emirates, Iraq and Iran are exported through this seaway each year. During the Iran–Iraq war of 1980–8 many oil tankers were sunk or damaged on their way to the West. Warships from the USA and a number of West European nations were sent into the Gulf to protect the tankers, and maintain their supply of oil.

Similar problems were faced when the Suez Canal was closed in 1956, as a strategic move by Egypt during wartime. Much of the UK's oil came through the canal from the Gulf, and as a result there was rationing of motor fuel in the UK at that time. In 1967, the canal was closed again, and after this there was a major programme to build much larger **supertankers** which carried crude oil to Western Europe by travelling round the southern tip of Africa. The size of the tankers made them much cheaper to run than earlier vessels, so although the sea route was much longer it was less costly.

Price changes

The price of crude oil and oil products varies enormously. For developed countries this makes it very difficult to estimate how much its raw materials for industry will cost. Increases in oil (fuel) prices mean increases in transport costs, which in turn usually mean increases in prices of many other items sold in shops or produced in factories. However, in developing countries a sharp increase in imported oil prices can be much more serious. Development plans can be held back several years if rising energy costs add to the imports bill of countries trying to build up their economies.

The Organisation of Petroleum Exporting Countries (OPEC) does try to control increases by fixing prices and production quotas for each member country. But these only have limited success. 14.5 shows some of the events which have affected petrol production and prices in recent years.

▼ 14.5 Petrol price changes

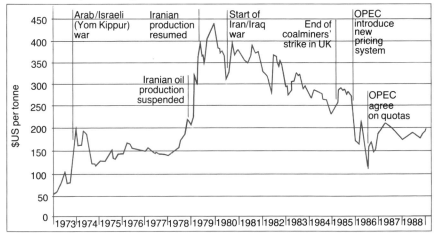

Oil and Natural Gas 63

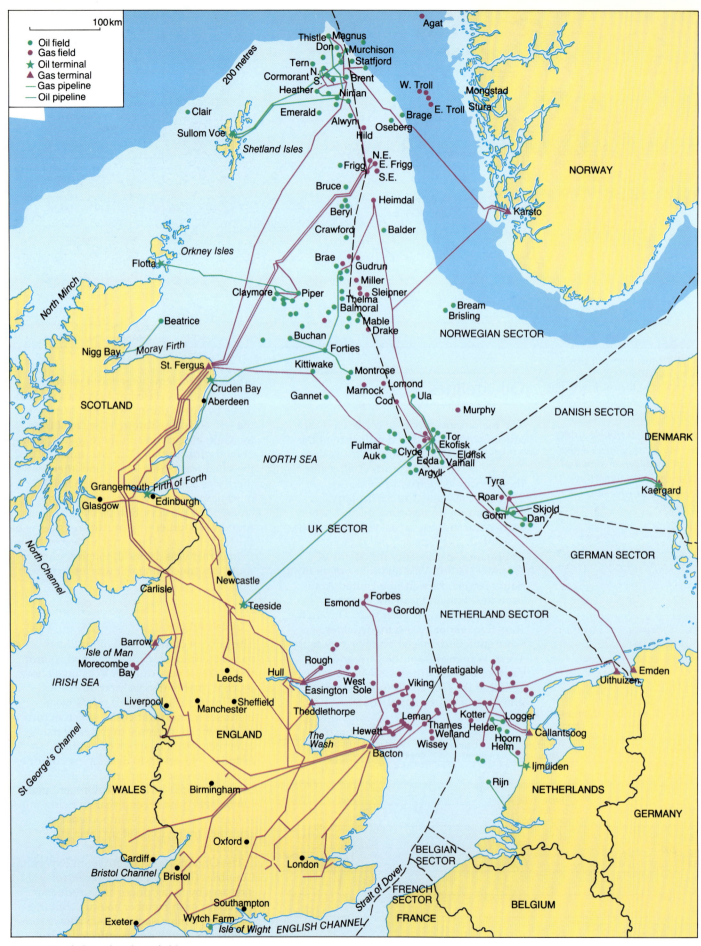

▲ 14.6 North Sea oil and gas fields

64 **Oil and Natural Gas**

North Sea Oil and Gas

During the 1950s and 1960s oil became increasingly popular in the UK. It was considered to be clean and efficient, and cheap supplies could be obtained from the Middle East. It had been known for some time that under the North Sea were rocks likely to contain oil and gas, and in 1959 a breakthrough occurred when a massive natural gas field was found at Slochteren (Netherlands). This encouraged exploration wells to be drilled in the North Sea.

Agreement was reached in 1964 about the ownership of the sea bed and its wealth, each country being allocated a sector (14.6). In 1965 the West Sole gas field was discovered, and numerous other finds followed. It was not until 1970 that the first major oilfield, Forties, was found, but from then on a series of fields were discovered.

Exploration in the Irish Sea found an important gas field in Morecambe Bay. Exploration continues all around Britain's coast, as well as on land.

Problems

The North Sea is one of the most difficult and dangerous areas in the world for exploration and production. New technology had to be developed to cope with the problems.

- The depth of the North Sea (80 to 200 metres) means that massive platforms had to be built.
- Many of the fields are over 100 km from land, and some are over 200 km.
- Weather conditions can often be very severe, ranging from very high winds with massive waves, to days-on-end when dense fog persists.
- The uneven sea bed makes pipe-laying very difficult.
- There has been opposition from conservation groups who fear that oil spillages will pollute the environment.

▲ 14.7 Oil rig

These problems have greatly increased the cost of building and maintaining oil and gas rigs, pipelines and terminals. The rigs are massive (14.7), and are supplied by helicopters and ships from the mainland. An increasing amount of oil is being moved to land by pipeline, though tankers also load from buoys in the North Sea (14.8). A whole system of natural gas pipelines now covers most of the UK, the major areas being shown in 14.6.

Benefits

14.9 shows that since 1981 the UK has produced more oil from the North Sea than it has consumed. This has allowed some to be sold for export, and has helped the UK's **trade balance** (the cost difference between imports and exports). How long the UK will remain self-sufficient will depend upon:

- the rate at which it exploits North Sea oil and finds new fields;
- the rate at which it consumes oil;
- the amount of oil it imports.

Industry has benefited from the employment that the development of the oil fields and shore terminals has brought. Just supplying the rigs with food and equipment employs between three and four times as many people as actually work on them. Employment and prosperity has been particularly brought to areas which had high unemployment and depopulation, for example Teeside, the Shetland Isles and north-east Scotland (especially Aberdeen).

Natural gas has replaced coal gas, and gives twice as much energy for a given amount. It is a very clean and efficient source of energy.

North Sea oil and gas have broadened the UK's energy base. This means that Britain is not dependent upon other countries for a large proportion of its supplies.

Make a table to show the benefits that North Sea oil and gas have brought. What strategy should the UK use in the future to make the best use of these resources?

▲ 14.8 Oil tanker loading from buoy

▼ 14.9 UK oil production

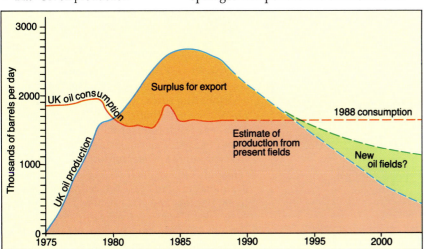

Oil and Natural Gas

▲ 14.10 Sullom Voe

Construct a table to show the gains and losses for Shetland Islanders as a result of North Sea oil. What measures can be taken in the future to prevent any long-term damage to their island and way of life?

▼ 14.11 Major refineries of the UK

▼ 14.12 Oil refining

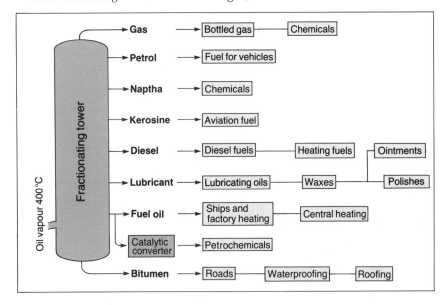

Sullom Voe

When the size of the oil fields in the North Sea became known, it was clear that so much oil would be produced that it would be impractical to rely solely on tankers to transport it from moored buoys. A number of shore terminals were therefore built (14.6).

Sullom Voe in the Shetland Islands is Europe's largest oil and liquified gas terminal (14.10). Crude oil from over a dozen oil fields is piped to the terminal, where excess water and gas is removed. Oil is then loaded onto tankers for delivery to refineries. The gas is liquified at very low temperature before it too is transported to the mainland.

The Shetland Islands offer the nearest land base to many of the largest UK oil fields, so were an obvious choice for locating a terminal. The site of Sullom Voe has a number of advantages:

- a deep-water channel allowing tankers of 100 000 tonnes (dead weight) to collect oil and gas;
- a sheltered harbour with sufficient space for very large tankers to manoeuvre;
- level land on which to build the terminal;
- virtually no other human activities, and away from the more densely populated areas of Shetland;
- land of little interest to the naturalist.

Attempts were made to ensure that development of facilities for the oil and gas industry were restricted to this one site, and it can now handle 75% of the UK's oil production.

However, the growth of the North Sea oil and gas industry has brought considerable change to the Shetland Isles, Orkney Isles and north-east Scotland.

- The highly paid jobs in the oil and gas industry have attracted people away from traditional industries, such as farming and fishing, increasing the depopulation of some areas.
- Although large numbers of workers were needed to build many of the facilities, fewer jobs are now needed to run them. For example to construct the Sullom Voe terminal involved 4800 workers, but running it needs only 850 people.
- A number of very quiet and beautiful rural areas have been transformed into industrial sites.
- A number of the oil fields are in rich fishing grounds, and fishing those areas has become difficult.
- There is a constant risk of oil spillage, which could have devastating effects on wildlife.

Refining

Tankers from the terminals, the oil fields and from other countries bring crude oil to oil refineries. The major UK refineries (14.11) are located on deep-water estuaries, or within relatively short pipeline distance of a deep-water terminal. There is also a need for large amounts of cooling water and large areas of flat land.

At the refinery the crude oil is processed to separate out the various products that it contains. The main process takes place in a **fractionating tower** and 14.12 shows the major products that result. Crude oil from a number of different sources is usually mixed to get the particular balance of the products that is required. Distribution of the wide range of refined products is expensive, so it is a major advantage if the refinery is close to its markets and has efficient road and rail networks. Chemical works are often located close to refineries to make use of products in the **petro-chemical industry**.

▲ 14.13 Booms surround the *Exxon Valdez*

Disaster in Alaska

Look at the information on this page about a major oil spillage in Alaska in 1989. Describe the effects of the spillage, and discuss the possible methods of dealing with the oil. What measures should be taken to prevent such a disaster occurring in the future?

5km off course the *Exxon Valdez* rips into a reef and spills 11 million gallons of crude oil

The great slick threatens a multitude of wildlife

▲ 14.14 Scene of the disaster

▶ 14.15 Marine life at risk

▼ 14.16 Dealing with the oil slick

Gales are wrecking attempts to stop America's biggest ever oil slick wiping out Alaska's teeming wildlife. As 100 km/h winds fanned the black tide over hundreds of square kilometres, Exxon Oil Chief Frank Iarossi said, "It's unbelievable, it's moving like it's on a super highway".

Exxon has been under attack for its bungled start in cleaning up the mess quickly, after the supertanker *Exxon Valdez* with only a junior crew member at the helm, ran onto a well-charted reef. Experts claim that Exxon's failure to take quick control of the situation has led to the needless pollution of many kilometres of beaches. However, some experts disagree about what to do next.

Spraying dispersant chemicals can seriously damage wildlife and, in the high winds, much has been blown off course. Burning the oil has also hit two major snags. The layer is now so thin that the almost freezing water beneath quickly douses any flames. And angry villagers in Tatitlek claim that the acrid smoke has caused nausea and severe headaches. The task force has also put out floating PVC barriers known as booms. But the oil has now spread so far that only the most sensitive beaches can be protected. Skimmers have also been used, but have had little success in the high winds.

Thousands of sea birds are already doomed to a cruel lingering death. Cleaning oiled feathers is hopeless when dealing with such large numbers of birds. Stocks of rare sea birds, otters, seals, whales, herring and salmon will all be decimated by poisoning and starvation.

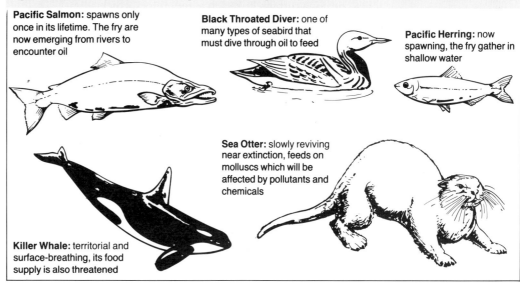

Pacific Salmon: spawns only once in its lifetime. The fry are now emerging from rivers to encounter oil

Black Throated Diver: one of many types of seabird that must dive through oil to feed

Pacific Herring: now spawning, the fry gather in shallow water

Sea Otter: slowly reviving near extinction, feeds on molluscs which will be affected by pollutants and chemicals

Killer Whale: territorial and surface-breathing, its food supply is also threatened

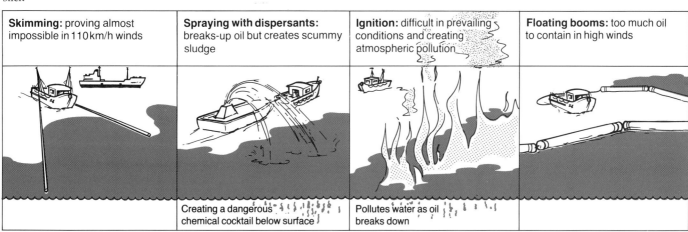

Skimming: proving almost impossible in 110 km/h winds

Spraying with dispersants: breaks-up oil but creates scummy sludge / Creating a dangerous chemical cocktail below surface

Ignition: difficult in prevailing conditions and creating atmospheric pollution / Pollutes water as oil breaks down

Floating booms: too much oil to contain in high winds

Oil and Natural Gas 67

15 Nuclear Power

Key idea
- There is considerable debate about the wisdom of developing nuclear power. Some believe it to be the energy of the future, while others claim that it will lead to environmental disaster.

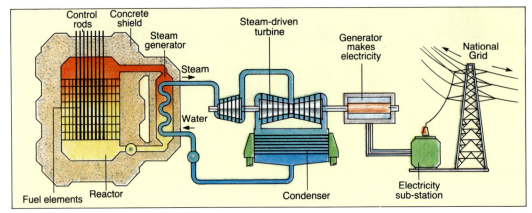

▶ 15.1 How a nuclear power station works

▼ 15.2 Wylfa power station

▼ 15.3 Nuclear power: top 20 countries

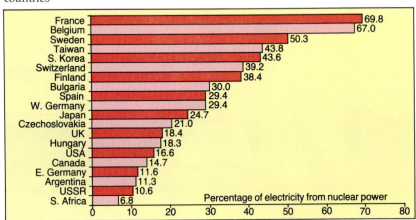

There are more arguments about nuclear power than any other energy source. In this unit both sides of the argument will be outlined in order to help you make up your own mind. 15.1 shows how a typical nuclear power station works. It is similar to any fossil fuel power station, in that water is heated to become steam. This steam then drives a turbine linked to a generator, which produces electricity to join the National Grid.

The heat required is produced in a nuclear reactor. Here uranium atoms inside special fuel rods are split in a controlled reaction called nuclear fission. This creates intense heat. To prevent dangerous radiation from escaping, the reactor is encased with a massive concrete shield. A modern reactor contains up to 100 tonnes of uranium, each tonne of which provides the same amount of energy as 20 000 tonnes of coal. 15.2 shows the nuclear power station at Wylfa on Anglesey in North Wales.

There are a variety of types of reactors, but potentially the most useful is the **fast breeder reactor**. These use plutonium (a material created from uranium) as a fuel. As the reaction takes place they 'breed' almost as much fuel as they use. If current research shows them to be a viable type of power station, they could possibly be the energy source of the future.

Rapid growth

World production of nuclear power has grown fast and now provides over a fifth of the electricity generated in developed countries. It has particularly grown as a replacement for oil, with the aim of reducing import costs. 15.3 shows the countries with the largest percentages of nuclear-powered electricity.

France has had a particularly large investment programme. With little of its own oil and natural gas, and a declining coal industry based on limited remaining reserves, nuclear power has been seen as the best way of providing cheap power. *The major arguments for developing nuclear power are shown in 15.4. List any others you can think of.*

▼ 15.4 Arguments for nuclear power

1. As oil and natural gas reserves decline there could be a serious energy shortage in the future.
2. Despite the high cost of building and running nuclear power stations, they may eventually produce the cheapest form of electricity.
3. Very little fuel (uranium) is needed, so transport costs are very low.
4. Relatively few workers are needed, so labour costs are low.
5. Nuclear power does not pollute the atmosphere with smoke or sulphur, unlike burning fossil fuels.
6. There has been a great investment in research, and there are many safeguards to make risks of an accident minimal.
7. Very little waste is involved and many people believe it can be stored safely.

68 Nuclear Power

▲ 15.5 Nuclear power in the UK

▼ 15.6 Disposal of nuclear waste

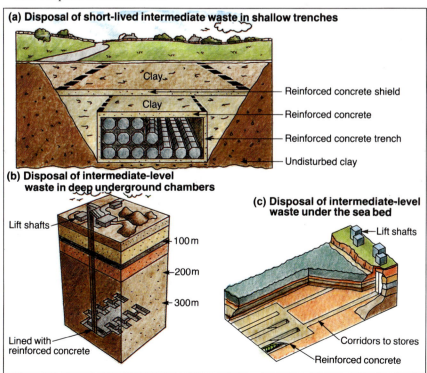

Nuclear Power in the UK

The UK was a pioneer in developing nuclear power: the world's first station to generate electricity for public consumption was opened in 1956 at Calder Hall in Cumbria. The stations now in operation (15.5) regularly produce over 20% of the UK's electricity.

The first nuclear power stations were built away from populated areas, in case of accidents where radioactivity was released. Most nuclear power stations are located

- on the coast, as vast quantities of water are needed for cooling;
- on areas with large amounts of flat land, if possible of low agricultural value;
- on strong geological foundations to take the massive weight of the reactor.
- away from areas with alternative energy supplies.

A number of locations, such as Hunterston, have two stations. There are also a number of smaller nuclear research establishments, some of which have reactors.

Nuclear waste

Some people think that the ideal nuclear energy source would be **nuclear fusion**. If scientists could control this process on a large scale, our energy problems might be solved because it produces less radioactive waste than **nuclear fission** does, and the fuel is water. (**Fission** means splitting atoms, **fusion** means joining them.) However, until then, society will face the problem of what to do with the waste that nuclear fission produces.

The waste is reprocessed, but that still means there are radioactive and potentially dangerous materials to dispose of. Some will stay radioactive for tens of thousands – even millions – of years, and so safe storage is essential. What is in dispute is whether we can be sure that anywhere will remain safe for that long. Also, what is *safe*? Some people believe that the safety levels currently in use allow people to come into contact with levels of radioactivity that will harm them or their children. There is argument over whether high rates of childhood leukaemia next to nuclear reprocessing plants have been caused by radioactivity from the plants. The nuclear industry, however, has claimed that it is not to blame.

Some low-level waste is discharged into the sea, but underground disposal sites are now being sought; the most suitable areas with clay-based rocks are shown in 15.5. A number of possible ways of disposing of the waste are shown in 15.6.

Nuclear Power 69

▲ 15.7 Nuclear death

▲ 15.8 Chernobyl

▼ 15.9 Exporting radiation

Accidents can Happen

15.7 shows that some people view nuclear power as a threat to human life. Undoubtedly the most important aspect of nuclear plant safety is to prevent the highly radioactive material in the core being released. But many serious accidents and radioactive releases have already occurred at nuclear plants.

- Windscale (now Sellafield, UK) 1957. Fuel in the reactor caught fire. Radioactivity contaminated large areas of farmland, millions of gallons of milk had to be disposed of, and estimates of deaths from cancer caused by the leak range from about 13 to over 1000.
- Three Mile Island (USA) 1979. A core meltdown destroyed the reactor. The clear-up is still continuing and has already cost well over $1 billion.
- Chernobyl (USSR) 1986. Control of the atomic chain reaction was lost. Vast amounts of heat were produced, causing an explosion, which destroyed the reactor (15.8). The core remained on fire for several days, and released a radioactive cloud that spread right across Europe (15.9).

The effects of Chernobyl

Immediate casualties: Hundreds, mostly around the plant, including over 30 firefighters who died after massive radiation exposure.

Cancers caused by radiation: 24000 to 500000 (estimates vary), which will take many years to show. These will include leukaemias (especially in children), body cancers and possible increases in Down's Syndrome.

Abortions: There was an increase in demand.

Evacuation: 135000 people evacuated from a zone within 30 km of the plant within eight days. Further evacuation took place from a zone 30 km to 80 km from the plant after these outlying regions were contaminated by radioactive fallout. Altogether an estimated 200000 were evacuated permanently, with another 450000 (mostly children and pregnant mothers) dispersed to holiday camps for the summer. The 30 km exclusion zone around Chernobyl will be enforced for the foreseeable future. There are no plans to resettle the inner 10 km zone.

Water supplies: Supplies to cities were threatened and had to be diverted.

Economic impact: About 50000 square kilometres of some of the best farming land in the USSR had to be taken out of production. The Soviet government put the cost of the disaster at $14 billion, but Western sources put it much higher.

Radiation: Massive impact beyond the USSR, with more radiation being released than from all the atomic bombs and nuclear tests ever exploded. Some individuals in the UK received a dose greater than one year's natural background radiation. Restrictions were placed on livestock in certain parts of Cumbria, Scotland and North Wales, affecting 3.5 million sheep on 8000 farms, and were still in force in 1990. In Scandinavia over 40000 contaminated reindeer have been slaughtered, badly affecting the way of life of the Lapp people.

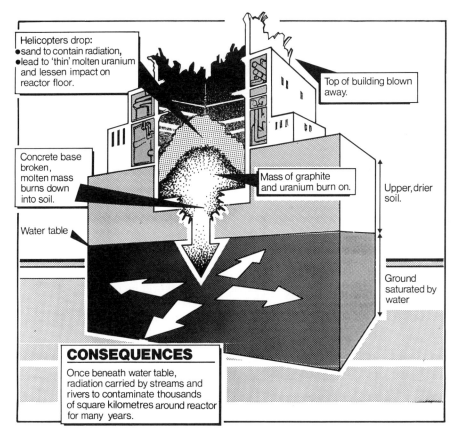

▲ 15.10 China syndrome

China syndrome

The worst did not happen at Chernobyl, and the fire was put out. But what is feared most is called the China syndrome (15.10). This is the nickname for an uncontrolled meltdown in a nuclear reactor. This would occur if there was a loss of the material cooling the reactor, and a failure of emergency systems. The molten nuclear reactor core, still generating immense heat, would fall through the floor of the reactor building, and burn its way down 'towards China' at the other side of the world.

Since Chernobyl, a number of people have changed their view about the risks of nuclear power. Certainly few people now consider that major accidents are so improbable that they are not worth bothering about. Instead there is an increasing acceptance that accidents will occur and the emphasis is now on ways of controlling their effects. The Science journal *Nature* wrote just after Chernobyl, 'The important question is not so much how accidents like these can be prevented, but how we can live with them safely.' Some members of the US 'Nuclear Regulators Commission' now estimate that the chances of a reactor in the USA suffering a core meltdown before 2000 are 50:50.

Too costly

Opponents of nuclear energy do not argue solely about the risks from an accident in the reactor. They are also convinced that it is impossible to store radioactive waste in a safe way for the thousands of years that it will remain dangerous. They feel that we are creating a great problem for future generations.

Doubts are also being expressed about whether nuclear power really is as cheap as its supporters claim. It was uncertainty over the economics of nuclear power that forced the British Government to withdraw all nuclear power stations from electricity privatisation plans in 1989. There have already been massive amounts of money spent on research, and the cost of decommissioning (closing down and making safe) nuclear power stations at the end of their lives is only just being realised. Storing radioactive waste will also be very costly. Some believe that if all of this money had been spent on alternative energy sources we would have new supplies of cheap energy today. They argue that energy conservation and renewable energy sources such as solar, wind and wave power could eventually provide the power we need.

Nuclear opponents are also convinced that estimates of the energy needed in the future have been exaggerated. Energy demand is now growing much less rapidly than in the 1970s, and there is no '**energy crisis**' in sight, as some thought there would be early in the next century.

Whether or not the views of nuclear opponents, summarised in 15.11, are all true, all countries except France had already seen a decline in the nuclear industry even before Chernobyl. In the USA not a single order for a nuclear reactor has been placed since 1977 without being cancelled soon after. Spain, Brazil and a number of other countries have also recently cancelled orders.

Consider all the information in this unit, both for and against nuclear power. You may even be able to organise a debate within your group. Outline your views about the future of the nuclear industry, giving your reasons.

▼ 15.11 Arguments against nuclear power

1. There will inevitably be more serious accidents, which will lead to deaths and ruin the environment for thousands of years.
2. There is no safe way of storing radioactive waste. We are causing major problems for future generations.
3. Energy demand is increasing less rapidly than was first thought likely in the 1970s. The world will have enough energy without nuclear power.
4. The cost of nuclear energy is very high, if all the costs of research, storing waste and decommissioning plants are included.
5. The money spent on research into nuclear power would be much more beneficial if spent developing other safer sources of energy.

16 Fuels of the Future?

Key idea
- As fossil fuels become more scarce, and as people become more aware of the environmental impact of their use, alternative sources of power are being sought.

Hydro-electric Power

In the early nineteenth century most industries in Europe and North America relied on waterpower. However, the development of the steam engine, which used coal, and later electricity, greatly reduced the importance of water as a power source. There is considerable potential for increasing the use of waterpower but, despite it being a renewable resource, it can cause environmental damage.

The best-known form of waterpower is hydro-electricity. Ideally a natural waterfall is used, but often a valley is dammed or a barrage is built across a river to create a **head of water**: a difference in height between two water levels (16.1). Water is then allowed to fall at great speed under the force of gravity through pipes called **penstocks**, running from the higher level to the power station at the lower level. Here, the fast-flowing water is used to drive the turbine blades inside the generator. In this way, the energy in the running water is turned into electricity, which is transmitted by transmission cables to the consumer.

Between 1960 and 1990 hydro-electric capacity in the world increased by over 300%. Even so, much of the potential of the world's rivers remains untapped. It has been calculated that, if all rivers were dammed, 50 times more hydro-electricity could be generated. This would be equal to about 12 000 nuclear reactors. Technical problems prevent all of this energy being harnessed, but it is considered possible to increase present production by 12 times.

Hydro-electric power is particularly attractive to countries that lack fossil fuels and have to import much of their fuel. For example Brazil hopes to generate 22 000 megawatts from the Amazon Basin by 2000. The Itaipu Dam on the Panama River can alone generate 12 600 megawatts, compared with a mere 1500 megawatts produced by most nuclear reactors.

However, large dams cause major environmental and social problems, which may far outweigh the benefits.

In the UK there are few suitable sites for hydro-electric stations, and in recent years only 1200 to 1400 megawatts have been produced. However, hydro power is the only practical system for the large-scale **storage** of electricity, as explained in 16.2.

▼ 16.1 Hydro-electric power

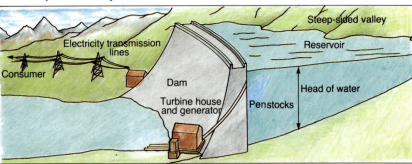

Europe's biggest pumped storage scheme was completed in 1983 at Dinorwic in North Wales. The idea is to use surplus electricity, particularly at night, to pump water up to a mountain top reservoir. This reservoir can then be emptied very quickly back down through the turbines to make electricity when demand is high. At Dinorwic 1800 megawatts can be generated for up to 5 hours from water stored 568 m above Lyn Peris.

▲ 16.2 Pumped storage, Dinorwic

▶ 16.3 Wave power

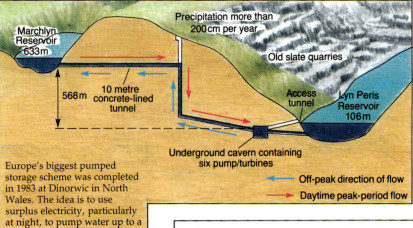

Wave Power

Sea waves are a potential renewable source of energy, by using their motion to make electricity. A number of devices have been invented and tested (16.3), but in the UK, where much of the early development took place, the Government recently withdrew funding for further development, preferring instead to increase the capacity of nuclear power generation. However, following their decision in 1989 to reduce support for future nuclear plants, due largely to their high cost, it is likely that wave power programmes may be looked at again.

Tidal Power

The pull of gravity from the sun and moon raises and lowers the level of the sea around the UK by 3 to 8 metres twice a day. These tides provide a huge amount of natural energy which could be harnessed. Already at Rance in Northern France a 750 metre long tidal barrage is producing cheap electricity by capturing tidal energy.

In such schemes a dam is built across an estuary which has a large tidal range. As the tide rises, tidal water is allowed to pass through the dam but is prevented from running back to the sea. The water behind the dam forms a reservoir. When the tide falls, the water from the reservoir is released, and used to turn turbines as it flows downstream. In some schemes there are two sets of turbines. One is operated by the rising tide, and the other by the water released at low tide.

The cost of building a tidal barrage is very high, but once it is completed operating costs are very low. Large amounts of power can be generated from a series of turbines. Provided that the bed behind the barrage is dredged regularly to prevent silt building up, the barrage should have a long life. The Severn Estuary in England is one of the most favourable sites in the world, and £4.5 million has just been spent investigating its potential (16.4). However, little is known about the long-term effects of such projects. The natural flow of water is interrupted, and vast quantities of silt may be trapped. Some wildlife may benefit while other species suffer.

▼ 16.4 Severn Estuary tidal power scheme

It's 16 kilometres long, costs £9 billion, will supply 7% of England and Wales' power and, like the Great Wall of China, is visible from space

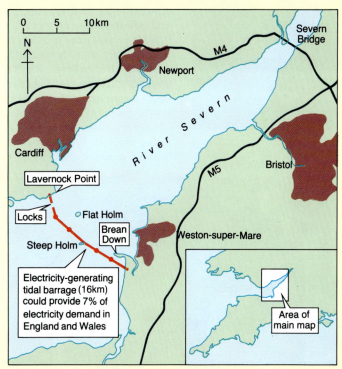

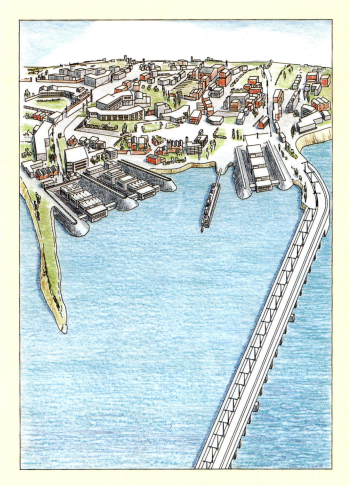

The plan takes advantage of one of the world's biggest tidal surges: the height of the Severn changes by over 8 metres a day. A massive artificial barrier 16 km long will be constructed, with a new dual carriageway road running across the top. Work could start by 1995.

The artist's impression on the left shows how the construction site could look when the barrage's giant turbines are assembled. The idea is that the barrage allows water to flood through as the tide is rising, until high tide when the flow is blocked. The water level on the other side of the barrage falls as the tide goes out, then the turbine gates are opened and the trapped water pours through. Power is generated as the released water hits the 9-metre long blades of the 216 submerged turbines. The turbines drive a generator from which electricity is fed into the National Grid.

Locks will allow ships up to 100 000 tonnes to pass through a channel 30 metres deep. Over 70 000 jobs will be created by the project. The scheme's designers claim that the barrage will create a haven for wildlife and watersports by reducing the turbulent currents. It will also be pollution free, cutting the amount of harmful carbon dioxide pumped into the air by traditional power stations by more than 17 million tonnes a year.

However, environmentalists fear that some wildlife will suffer, and have given the proposals a lukewarm reception. The major problem is that the Severn is rather muddy. There are at least 10 million tonnes of fine sediment in suspension, extensive inter-tidal mudflats, and vast areas of unstable mud on the sea bed. If the barrage is built, some areas will benefit as marine creatures will colonise areas where silt settles out, and this will benefit other wildlife. However, some mudflats favoured by thousands of wading birds will be permanently flooded. Much more research is needed to determine the possible environmental damage before the scheme is approved.

List the points for and against the scheme, and suggest what further investigations should be carried out before it is approved.

Fuels of the Future?

▼ 16.5 Solar panels on satellite

Solar Power

The total amount of energy reaching the earth from the sun is enormous, but it is difficult to harness it in an economical way. If this can be done, it will provide virtually limitless, safe, and pollution-free energy.

Solar panels now provide electricity for almost every satellite (16.5). They use solar cells, which convert sunlight directly into electricity. There are ideas for harnessing much larger amounts of power in this way in a solar power station. This would be a power station in space with solar panels always facing the sun. The power would then be beamed down to stations on the earth.

At the earth's surface, large areas of solar panels are needed to produce useful amounts of electricity (16.6). The investment cost is very high. Solar energy can also be tapped using many mirrors which follow the sun's path and reflect sunlight continuously onto a boiler. This makes steam which can then generate electricity. However, the potential use of such plants is limited by the amount of sunlight received. In countries such as the UK, there are very few sunshine hours during the winter when energy needs are the greatest. However, in tropical developing countries, even small schemes can be extremely valuable.

At the present time, research is concentrating on the development of a **photovoltaic cell**. This is a method of using the sun's energy to make electricity, even when it is cloudy, without producing heat. Photovoltaic cells are still too expensive for general use, but as research continues their price should fall, allowing them to compete with conventional energy sources.

One of the best ways of using solar energy in countries such as the UK is to make houses into solar heat traps (16.7). Such houses cost 5–10% more to build, but reduce heating bills by 50–75%. Many of the ideas can also be incorporated into conventional houses. *Consider your home. How could it make better use of free solar energy?*

▼ 16.6 Solar power station

▼ 16.7 A solar-heated house

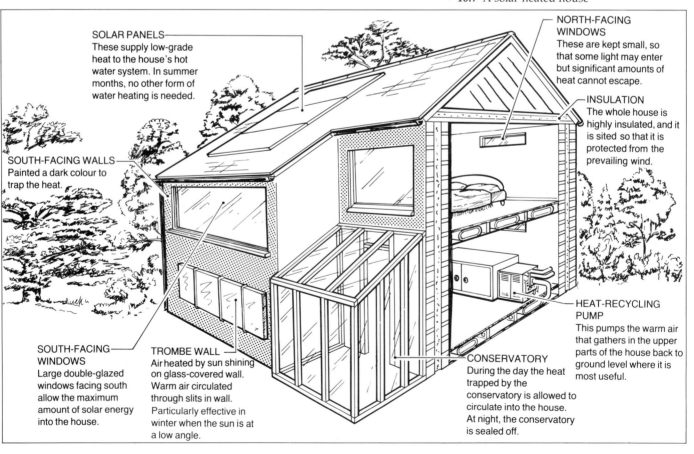

SOLAR PANELS — These supply low-grade heat to the house's hot water system. In summer months, no other form of water heating is needed.

SOUTH-FACING WALLS — Painted a dark colour to trap the heat.

SOUTH-FACING WINDOWS — Large double-glazed windows facing south allow the maximum amount of solar energy into the house.

TROMBE WALL — Air heated by sun shining on glass-covered wall. Warm air circulated through slits in wall. Particularly effective in winter when the sun is at a low angle.

NORTH-FACING WINDOWS — These are kept small, so that some light may enter but significant amounts of heat cannot escape.

INSULATION — The whole house is highly insulated, and it is sited so that it is protected from the prevailing wind.

CONSERVATORY — During the day the heat trapped by the conservatory is allowed to circulate into the house. At night, the conservatory is sealed off.

HEAT-RECYCLING PUMP — This pumps the warm air that gathers in the upper parts of the house back to ground level where it is most useful.

Fuels of the Future?

▼ 16.8 Wind farm, Hawaii

Wind Power

Windmills designed to harness the energy of the wind first appeared around 4000 years ago in China and Japan. However, only since the 1940s has wind power been used to make electricity. Modern devices use rigid blades rather than sails and owe much to the use of lightweight materials and advances in research, particularly in the design of the rotor blades.

Individual machines vary in size from those designed to produce a few kilowatts for a family or farm, to large models intended to serve whole communities, or to feed into a grid network. Economically it is usually better to have a large number of small machines grouped together in a **wind farm** (16.8), than to have a few very large ones.

The USA leads the world's development of wind power, and 95% of the world's present wind power capacity comes from California alone. Some 16 000 machines in the USA supply 1500 megawatts of power. At the other extreme, China has concentrated on much smaller machines: its 17 000 machines supply 1.7 megawatts.

Within the UK it has been estimated that if large wind turbines were installed on every suitable windy hill top, they could produce 7% of the UK's electricity needs. However, there would be environmental objections to many of these sites, and it is likely that only around 25% of them could be developed. Wind farms built in shallow water just offshore could be more promising, contributing up to 15% of our electricity needs at a cheaper price than conventional sources. Such schemes are particularly suitable for remote communities, especially on islands such as the Orkneys, where some wind turbines have already been sited.

16.9 shows data about an experimental 1000 kilowatt machine built at Richborough in Kent. Power is only produced when wind speed reaches 6 metres per second, and full power is reached at 13 metres per second. The wind distribution diagram shows how often these figures are likely to be achieved. As a result it is estimated that the machine will only produce 22% of what it could produce if operated continuously. This also makes it clear that wind power will need to be used with other sources of energy, for on some days the wind will not blow!

List the advantages and disadvantages of wind and geothermal power. Which do you think is likely to be of greatest importance in the future?

▼ 16.9 Richborough wind turbine

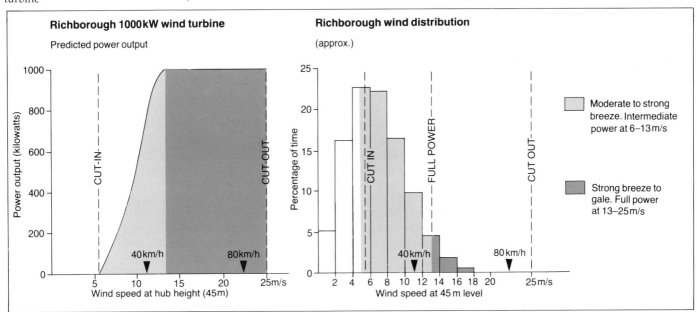

▼ 16.10 Geothermal station at Lake Myvatn, Iceland

Geothermal Power

In some places hot underground rocks can be found quite near the earth's surface, and this heat can be used in a variety of ways. Where water flows through the rock naturally, and becomes hot, it can be used immediately, either to heat buildings, or to make steam to generate electricity. More often, boreholes have to be drilled, rocks fractured by deep explosions, and cold water pumped down. Once heated, this water can be pumped to the surface (16.10).

Geothermal energy may only ever make a small contribution to the world's energy supplies, because few areas are suitable for its generation. Also, production costs are high, and the very hot water may be acidic, and so damage equipment and borehole linings. However, in favourable areas it can be important. Nicaragua already gains more than 50% of its energy from geothermal sources. Geothermal power is also making major contributions in New Zealand, Iceland, Indonesia, the USSR and Mexico.

Fuels of the Future?

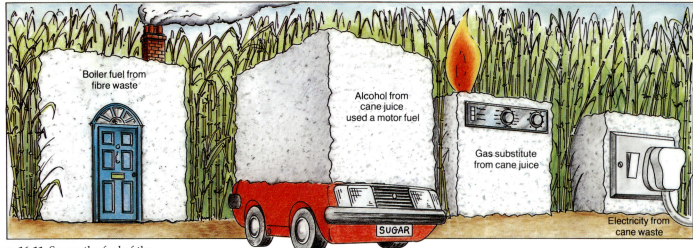

▲ 16.11 Sugar: the fuel of the future

▼ 16.12 Power from plants

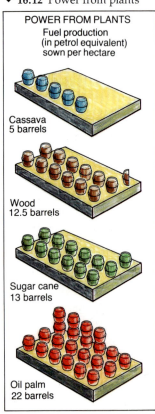

Biomass Power

Energy produced from plant and animal matter (**biomass energy**) is becoming increasingly important. It is particularly being used in developing countries that have previously relied on expensive imported oil.

Brazil has one of the largest programmes; 16.11 shows a number of ways in which the waste products from producing sugar from sugar cane are used. Plants are a very effective way of using the most abundant source of free energy: the sun. By means of photosynthesis they convert solar energy into energy-rich plant material. The tropical grasses, including sugar cane, are among the most efficient.

Brazil now has over 2 million vehicles which use alcohol made from sugar cane juice instead of petrol; 9 million vehicles run on a mixture of 20% alcohol and 80% petrol. The fibrous waste from the sugar cane plant has around 70% of the heat value of wood, and is burnt to provide the energy to power the sugar mills. In Hawaii and South Africa, sugar factories sell energy to the National Grid.

Various research groups are looking at ways of gaining even more energy from plants like sugar. 16.12 shows a number of the most promising. Selective breeding has produced rapidly growing new varieties of sugar cane. **Energy cane** will produce an average of 315 tonnes of biomass per hectare each year compared with 60–100 tonnes from ordinary cane.

There is also much promising research into the use of animal and human waste. If human and animal sewage is stored in a **digester**, it ferments to produce a methane-rich gas. Such systems also dispose of sewage, and provide free fertiliser.

Rubbish

In the UK, rubbish could be used to produce heat and power for 2½ million homes, factories, schools and hospitals. New jobs could be created, unsightly waste tips closed down, precious fossil fuels conserved and pollution drastically reduced. 16.13 shows two ways in which rubbish can be used to make energy. More information on rubbish as a fuel is given on page 50.

▼ 16.13 Rubbish as a fuel

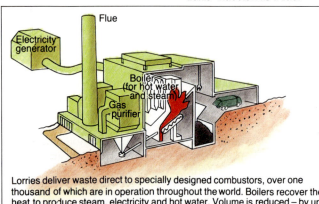

Lorries deliver waste direct to specially designed combustors, over one thousand of which are in operation throughout the world. Boilers recover the heat to produce steam, electricity and hot water. Volume is reduced – by up to 95% after metal recovery – leaving a sterile residue which can be safely tipped or used for construction.

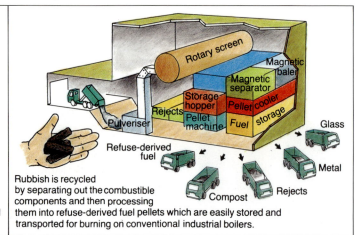

Rubbish is recycled by separating out the combustible components and then processing them into refuse-derived fuel pellets which are easily stored and transported for burning on conventional industrial boilers.

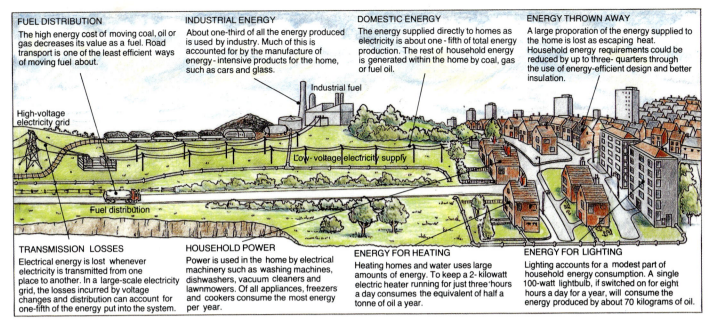

▲ 16.14 How energy is used

FUEL DISTRIBUTION
The high energy cost of moving coal, oil or gas decreases its value as a fuel. Road transport is one of the least efficient ways of moving fuel about.

INDUSTRIAL ENERGY
About one-third of all the energy produced is used by industry. Much of this is accounted for by the manufacture of energy-intensive products for the home, such as cars and glass.

DOMESTIC ENERGY
The energy supplied directly to homes as electricity is about one-fifth of total energy production. The rest of household energy is generated within the home by coal, gas or fuel oil.

ENERGY THROWN AWAY
A large proportion of the energy supplied to the home is lost as escaping heat. Household energy requirements could be reduced by up to three-quarters through the use of energy-efficient design and better insulation.

TRANSMISSION LOSSES
Electrical energy is lost whenever electricity is transmitted from one place to another. In a large-scale electricity grid, the losses incurred by voltage changes and distribution can account for one-fifth of the energy put into the system.

HOUSEHOLD POWER
Power is used in the home by electrical machinery such as washing machines, dishwashers, vacuum cleaners and lawnmowers. Of all appliances, freezers and cookers consume the most energy per year.

ENERGY FOR HEATING
Heating homes and water uses large amounts of energy. To keep a 2-kilowatt electric heater running for just three hours a day consumes the equivalent of half a tonne of oil a year.

ENERGY FOR LIGHTING
Lighting accounts for a modest part of household energy consumption. A single 100-watt lightbulb, if switched on for eight hours a day for a year, will consume the energy produced by about 70 kilograms of oil.

▼ 16.15 Fuel-hungry house

Six ways to make a house more energy-efficient

- **Insulate the loft.** One of the simplest ways of saving energy. In the average house, a 100 mm layer of loft insulation will pay for itself in three years.
- **Fit double-glazing.** A fairly expensive way of saving energy. Secondary glazing can usually be fitted to existing windows, and will save energy almost as well.
- **Insulate cavity walls.** This will save a considerable amount of energy.
- **Draughtproof doors and windows.** Will usually pay for itself within two years. Care is needed if your house contains any fuel-burning heaters without external flues: these need good ventilation.
- **Insulate tanks and pipes.** Fitting a 10-centimetre jacket around a hot-water cylinder is the most effective way of preventing energy loss.
- **Fit radiator thermostats.** Radiators can be made more efficient by installing individual thermostats and fitting foil to reflect heat from external walls behind them.

The Fifth Fuel

The Association for the Conservation of Energy call their magazine *The Fifth Fuel* to emphasise that conserving energy could save as much fuel as we could gain by finding another major type to add to coal, oil, natural gas and nuclear power. As a country the UK is near the bottom of the international league when it comes to the careful use of energy, 16.14 shows some of the most obvious ways in which people are wasteful. A number of points are particularly important.

- It makes very little sense to use electricity for heating. Over 80% of the heat contained in the fuel used in power stations is wasted in making the electricity, transmitting it, and by inefficient heating appliances. In contrast, fuels burnt in homes or factories can give up to 70–80% of their energy content as useful heat. Only about 5% of our delivered energy needs to be in the form of electricity, yet we are encouraged to use it in a very wasteful way.

- Many homes are so poorly designed that they lose up to 75% of the heat energy used (16.15). Although modern houses are, to an extent, designed with energy conservation in mind, truly energy-efficient houses are a rarity. It must also be noted that not all energy saved in homes will result in less energy being used. About two-thirds of energy saved is usually taken up by people increasing their level of comfort; only around one-third results in a cut in energy consumption. *Find out how your home and school score in terms of their energy efficiency.*

- The major energy producers are all competing for a larger share of the energy market, and so encourage us to use more energy. Often they encourage us to use their type of energy in a very wasteful way, and of course they then benefit from greater profits. In many countries there is a **coordinated energy policy**, with consumers being encouraged to use less and to use the particular source which is most efficient for a particular job.

- Although industry has already made some savings, it has been calculated that it could cut its energy bill by 30% if more energy conservation measures were taken.

What do you think should be done? How would you try to encourage people to use energy more wisely? Would you control the energy producers and energy production in any way?

Badly fitting windowframes — North-facing windows — Uninsulated loft — Single glazing — Inefficient boiler — Unlagged pipes — uninsulated walls — Inefficient radiators

Fuels of the Future?

17 Managing the Oceans

Key ideas
- The oceans hold a vast store of resources some of which we have hardly begun to tap.
- Our conflicting demands on, and lack of care for, the oceans could lead to the squandering of these resources, and severe damage to ourselves and other living creatures.

The oceans cover 71% of the earth's surface, and for the most part they have barely been explored. If the oceans' resources are to be managed effectively, much greater care will be needed than is being shown at present.

Ownership of the sea bed within 320 km (200 miles) of land is given to the nearest country. Disputes may occur when there is doubt about the ownership of isolated, and often uninhabited, islands, resulting in huge areas of the sea bed being claimed by several nations.

17.1 shows that the USA has by far the largest share of the sea bed, and that in general it is developed countries that own the largest areas. Outside the 320 km zones no country can claim ownership, and international conferences decide what should happen.

A major problem is that we are putting conflicting demands upon the oceans, particularly the shallow continental shelves around our coasts (17.2). We are trying to harness the sea for food, mine its minerals, use it as a rubbish dump, and enjoy it in our leisure time. The present inefficient management cannot continue if we want the oceans to survive as a valuable resource and home to a variety of wildlife.

Fisheries supply 23% of the world's protein and a livelihood for millions of people. However, world fish stocks are now threatened, particularly by overfishing. In some parts of the North Atlantic herring have been fished to the verge of extinction, while stocks of Atlantic cod, haddock and capelin have been greatly reduced. In the South Atlantic, pilchard catches have fallen drastically. In the Pacific, anchovy, salmon, halibut and a number of other species have been overfished.

Pollution has also destroyed many fisheries. In the UK the Humber estuary used to support a thriving fishing industry. Now it is dead as a result of industrial pollution. In the USA fish stocks in Chesapeake Bay have been all but destroyed by pollution; oysters and bass have been particularly badly hit. Coastal fisheries in many other countries have been affected in a similar way.

Unless action is taken soon to ease the pressure on fish stock, the prospects for the world's fisheries could be disastrous.

USA	12.48
France	7.4
Australia	6.23
Indonesia	4.06
New Zealand	3.65
United Kingdom	3.47
Canada	3.34
USSR	3.26
Japan	2.92
Brazil	2.38
Mexico	2.14

▲ 17.1 World's largest 320 km zones (million km²)

▼ 17.2 Conflicting demands on the ocean

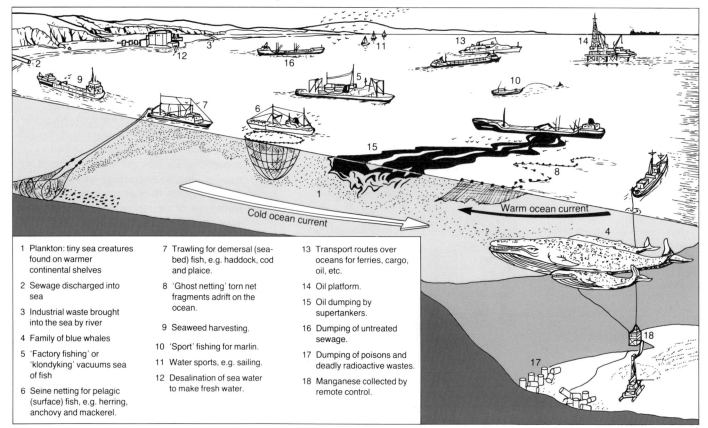

1. Plankton: tiny sea creatures found on warmer continental shelves
2. Sewage discharged into sea
3. Industrial waste brought into the sea by river
4. Family of blue whales
5. 'Factory fishing' or 'klondyking' vacuums sea of fish
6. Seine netting for pelagic (surface) fish, e.g. herring, anchovy and mackerel.
7. Trawling for demersal (sea-bed) fish, e.g. haddock, cod and plaice.
8. 'Ghost netting' torn net fragments adrift on the ocean.
9. Seaweed harvesting.
10. 'Sport' fishing for marlin.
11. Water sports, e.g. sailing.
12. Desalination of sea water to make fresh water.
13. Transport routes over oceans for ferries, cargo, oil, etc.
14. Oil platform.
15. Oil dumping by supertankers.
16. Dumping of untreated sewage.
17. Dumping of poisons and deadly radioactive wastes.
18. Manganese collected by remote control.

▼ 17.3 Fish farming near Inverary, Scotland

Fishing Controls

To protect fish stocks, a variety of measures have been taken in a number of the main fishing grounds. The EC's Common Fisheries Policy (CFP) is one example.

- Fishing rights. With a number of small exceptions, individual member countries have exclusive fishing rights within 19 km (12 miles) of their coasts. Overall the EC claims rights within 320 km (200 miles) of all member countries' coasts. Within this zone any member country can fish.
- Conserving stocks. Each country is given a quota of fish that it is allowed to catch each year. The quotas are calculated by estimating the total quantities of each species that can safely be caught, and then giving each member a share which reflects the proportion of stocks that it has caught in the past. Certain fishing grounds have been closed altogether, or at certain times of the year, to allow stocks to build up. There are also controls on the mesh sizes of the nets, so that smaller fish are allowed to escape.
- Financial help. Subsidies are used to maintain fish prices, and grants are given when boats have to stop fishing because quotas have been met.

Such measures are often very unpopular, and many fishermen have been put out of business. However, skippers are required by law to keep a record of all of their catches, and each member country must take legal action against those who break the agreements.

Despite the problems of the CFP it is a beginning. Many conservationists believe that the next step should be a whole-world fishing policy.

Aquaculture

Aquaculture, or the farming of fish, mussels, oysters and other aquatic creatures is now being actively promoted by the UN Food and Agriculture Organisation (FAO). They see it as a new source of fish supplies for many developing countries. At present it accounts for about 15% of world fish production, and FAO would like to see this increasing by at least five times by the year 2000.

Most production at present comes from small holders using traditional fish farming techniques (17.3). Such systems are cheap to run, use simple technology and use existing sites such as village ponds, paddy fields and irrigation canals. Fish farming fits into the local economy, and the fish are available to the local people.

However, the schemes supported by FAO are very large scale, use very modern technology, and rely on a high degree of capital investment. The fish produced are expensive, and usually sent to urban markets or for export. There is a shortage of suitable sites. Aquaculture requires a fertile clay soil and a reliable gravity-fed supply of clean water. Often the only places available are on land that is valuable for agriculture and already in use.

It is therefore unlikely that there will be a major increase in aquaculture in the near future. *Do you think that large-scale schemes will help to feed the poor in developing countries?*

Sea Bed Mining

As yet we have only begun to explore the narrow continental shelves around our shores. But it is likely that a whole range of valuable minerals are to be found in the ocean depths. Of particular interest are mineral nodules found at great depths on the sea bed. 17.4 shows how these could be mined, and gives some examples of deposits estimated to be in the Pacific Ocean alone.

▼ 17.4 Riches from the sea bed

Land above sea = 29%
Land beneath sea = 71% of the earth
Average depth 5000m
Continental shelf — Continental slope — Abyss or Ocean Floor

Examples from the Pacific:

Mineral	Deposit (billion tonnes)	Potential supply (in years) SEA	LAND
Aluminium	43.0	20 000	100
Manganese	358.0	400 000	100
Copper	7.9	6 000	40
Nickel	14.7	150 000	100
Cobalt	5.2	200 000	40

Mineral-bearing nodules abound on sea bed
They are up to 25cm long and shaped like potatoes
Nodules contain:
Manganese   Titanium
Aluminium   Molybdenum
Copper   Zirconium
Nickel   Vanadium
Cobalt   Lead
Iron

Managing the Oceans

▼ 17.5 The North Sea: sources of UK pollution

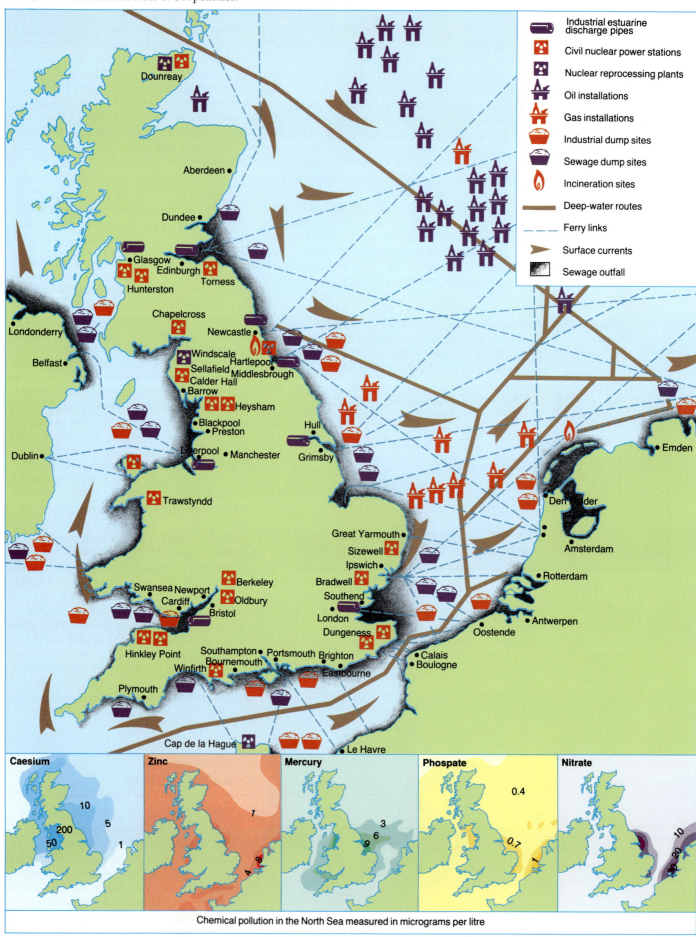

Chemical pollution in the North Sea measured in micrograms per litre

80 **Managing the Oceans**

Poisoning the Oceans

17.5 shows a wide variety of ways in which we are poisoning the oceans. The North Sea is only one example from many.

- Dumping. The UK dumps over 4 million tonnes of industrial waste, 13 million tonnes of contaminated sewage sludge, and 5 million tonnes of dredged material into the sea each year. The UK is responsible for 75% of all industrial waste and 99% of all sewage waste dumped into the North Sea.
- Burning hazardous waste on incinerator ships. Already banned in the Mediterranean and Baltic Seas, this still continues in the North Sea.
- Oil spillage. Some 400 000 tonnes of oil a year is spilled into the North Sea, most from discharges from the land.
- Discharging. Grossly polluted rivers discharge huge quantities of oil, sewage and industrial waste into the North Sea each year.
- Beaches. Many of our most famous bathing beaches do not reach EC standards of cleanliness. Blackpool is one of the most polluted.
- Shipping hazardous waste. Over 125 000 ships pass through the Straits of Dover each year, making the North Sea the busiest shipping area in the world. Many ships carry oil and some very poisonous material, which if spilled could cause a major environmental disaster.
- Radioactive leaks. It has been claimed that cooling water from nuclear power stations and leaks from a number of plants have caused radiation to rise to dangerous levels in some coastal areas.

Wildlife: who cares?

The dual attack on wildlife from overfishing and pollution has had serious effects in some areas. Whales have been particularly badly hit: 17.6 shows how the various species have declined. As most whaling is carried out in international waters, outside the national 320 km limits, it is particularly difficult to control. Most decisions are taken by the International Whaling Commission (IWC) although it has no powers to make countries obey its decisions.

In 1982 the IWC voted to impose a five-year ban on whaling from October 1985. However, a number of countries, notably the USSR, Japan, South Korea, Norway and Iceland, exploited loopholes in the new rules which allow whales to be killed for scientific research. For example, in 1986 Japan killed 1941 minke whales and 400 sperm whales. In 1987 Japan announced that it intended to kill for research purposes some 825 minke whales and 50 sperm whales each year for the next twelve years. Only threats from the USA to reduce Japan's fishing quota in US waters made Japan agree to cut its catches to only 300 minke and no sperm whales. But, unless firm rules are followed by all, the whales will remain in danger.

Around our coasts porpoises, dolphins and seals are all at risk. Thousands of sea birds and many other sea creatures are also killed each year, and some species are endangered.

Describe the ways in which the North Sea is being polluted. Are some areas more badly affected than others?

Does it matter that our management of the oceans seems to be so poor? What do you think should be done?

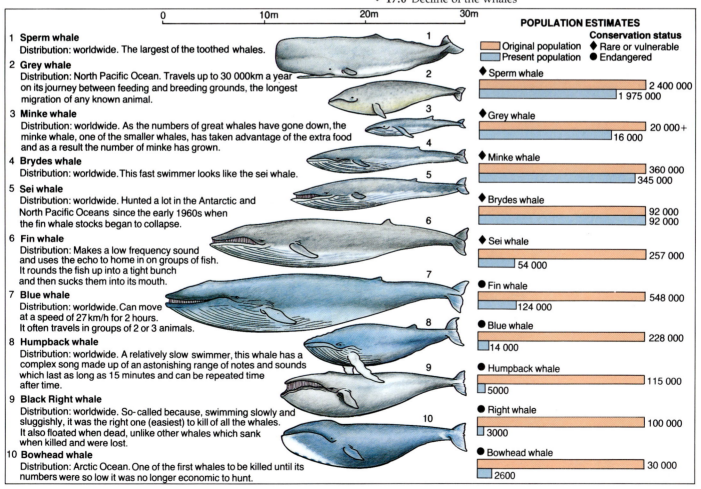

▼ 17.6 Decline of the whales

1 Sperm whale
Distribution: worldwide. The largest of the toothed whales.

2 Grey whale
Distribution: North Pacific Ocean. Travels up to 30 000km a year on its journey between feeding and breeding grounds, the longest migration of any known animal.

3 Minke whale
Distribution: worldwide. As the numbers of great whales have gone down, the minke whale, one of the smaller whales, has taken advantage of the extra food and as a result the number of minke has grown.

4 Brydes whale
Distribution: worldwide. This fast swimmer looks like the sei whale.

5 Sei whale
Distribution: worldwide. Hunted a lot in the Antarctic and North Pacific Oceans since the early 1960s when the fin whale stocks began to collapse.

6 Fin whale
Distribution: Makes a low frequency sound and uses the echo to home in on groups of fish. It rounds the fish up into a tight bunch and then sucks them into its mouth.

7 Blue whale
Distribution: worldwide. Can move at a speed of 27 km/h for 2 hours. It often travels in groups of 2 or 3 animals.

8 Humpback whale
Distribution: worldwide. A relatively slow swimmer, this whale has a complex song made up of an astonishing range of notes and sounds which last as long as 15 minutes and can be repeated time after time.

9 Black Right whale
Distribution: worldwide. So-called because, swimming slowly and sluggishly, it was the right one (easiest) to kill of all the whales. It also floated when dead, unlike other whales which sank when killed and were lost.

10 Bowhead whale
Distribution: Arctic Ocean. One of the first whales to be killed until its numbers were so low it was no longer economic to hunt.

POPULATION ESTIMATES

Conservation status:
- Original population
- Present population
- ◆ Rare or vulnerable
- ● Endangered

Species	Original	Present	Status
◆ Sperm whale	2 400 000	1 975 000	Rare or vulnerable
◆ Grey whale	20 000+	16 000	Rare or vulnerable
◆ Minke whale	360 000	345 000	Rare or vulnerable
◆ Brydes whale	92 000	92 000	Rare or vulnerable
◆ Sei whale	257 000	54 000	Rare or vulnerable
● Fin whale	548 000	124 000	Endangered
● Blue whale	228 000	14 000	Endangered
● Humpback whale	115 000	5000	Endangered
● Right whale	100 000	3000	Endangered
● Bowhead whale	30 000	2600	Endangered

Managing the Oceans

18 Environmental Decisions

Key ideas
- As a result of our careless management, the earth faces environmental disaster.
- We have sufficient knowledge to solve most of the problems that we have created, but it is much less certain that we have the will to make the changes in our lifestyles that will be necessary.

An increasing number of people now believe that we have reached an important crossroads in human history. Our careless management of the earth has created a range of environmental problems that could easily destroy all human and most other life. We have the scientific knowledge to solve most of the problems that we have caused, but are we prepared to make the changes in our lifestyles and bear the financial cost that will be needed to save the planet?

Acid Rain

The scale of acid rain pollution is vast, and it is truly a world problem (18.1). All the countries of Europe are involved, some contributing heavily to the burden of acidity, others receiving more than their fair share as the pollution is carried by winds across land and sea. The UK exports much of its pollution on prevailing westerly winds, but it is beginning to suffer increasingly from acid pollution itself.

Acid rain is produced from a complicated mixture of air pollutants which come mostly from burning fossil fuels (18.2). The main ingredients are sulphur and nitrogen oxides (SO_2 and NO_x). These gases undergo chemical changes in the atmosphere and fall as sulphuric and nitric acids (H_2SO_4 and HNO_3) in rain, mist and snow. Hydrocarbons, which come mostly from car exhausts, also play a damaging part. These cause smogs, and chemical changes in sunlight increase the presence of photochemicals, particularly ozone (O_3). Ozone itself is poisonous to trees, and helps to speed up the chemical changes which turn sulphates and nitrates into soluble acids. In addition to acid rain, there is also dry deposition, which deposits these chemicals closer to where they were formed.

Highly acid rain has been falling over much of Europe for over 100 years. It is now estimated that 20 million tonnes of sulphur dioxide and 9 million tonnes of nitrogen oxides enter the atmosphere over Western Europe each year. Acidity is measured on the pH scale which ranges from 0 to 14 (18.3).

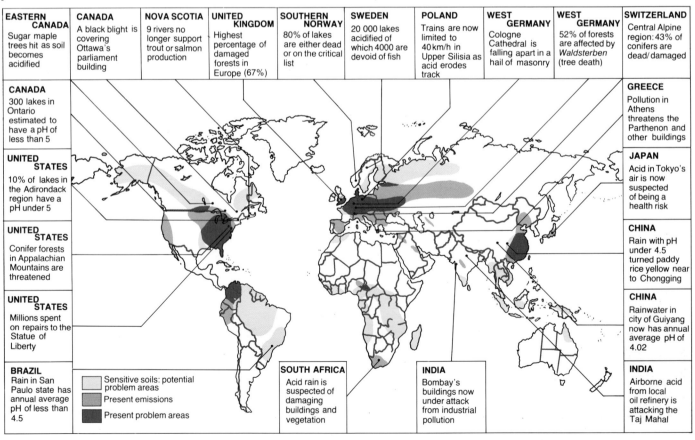

▼ 18.1 Acid rain: a world problem

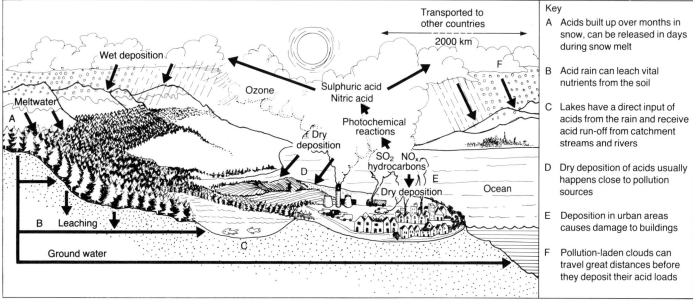

▲ 18.2 Acid pollution cycle

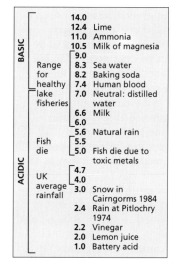

▲ 18.3 pH values

It is a **logarithmic** scale, which means that a change of 1 unit represents a ten fold change. Thus a solution of pH 3 is ten times more acidic than one of pH 4, 100 times more acidic than one of pH 5, and so on. Natural rain has an acidity level of 5.6.

▼ 18.5 Forest damage

Effects

- **Lakes and rivers**: in areas where the bedrocks weather slowly and do not contain lime, acid levels have built up. Damage starts when the pH of the water is less than 6.5; and all normal life dies if the pH falls below 5. 18.4 shows how the long accumulation of excess acidity has affected acidity levels of lakes, rivers and streams in Europe.
- **Forests**: acid rain leaches away nutrients from the soil, particularly calcium and potassium. Although many trees can withstand acid conditions, ozone poisons them, and is probably responsible for much of the damage often blamed on acid rain (18.5).
- **Crops**: yield loss of 10–20% occurs in the worst-affected areas.
- **Ground water**: as acid water percolates downwards it concentrates in underground supplies. 20% of Sweden's wells are now acidified, and water pipes are corroding.
- **Buildings**: acid corrosion is eating away metal, stone and wood in many cities. Historic buildings are in danger.
- **Health**: cancer has been linked to many of the chemicals contained within dry and wet acid deposition. Acid mists and smogs (often ten times more acidic than acid rain) are common throughout Europe, particularly affecting people with asthma and bronchitis.

Solutions

- **Cut vehicle emissions**: by improving public transport, reducing speed limits, and fixing catalytic converters to exhaust systems.

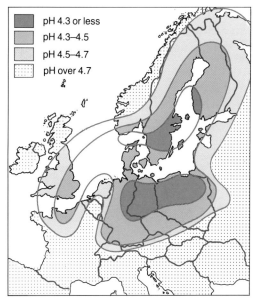

▲ 18.4 Acid rainfall: surface water acidification

- **Cut SO_2 and NO_x emissions from power stations**: 95% could be cut by removing the sulphur from coal before burning, using more efficient burning techniques, and scrubbing waste gases with ammonium and calcium compounds before they are released.
- **Using energy wisely**: two-thirds of all energy produced by burning fossil fuels is wasted. Much could be saved by energy conservation measures. Environmentally friendly energy sources should be developed.

These measures will cost money, but do we have a choice? Even if we introduce them it will take time to reduce acid levels, and so short-term measures such as the liming of lakes are also needed.

Environmental Decisions

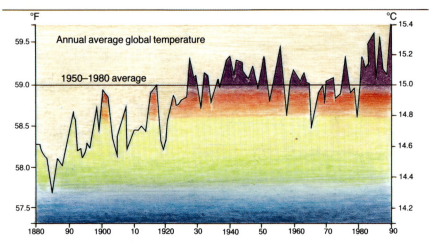

▲ 18.6 Increasing world temperatures

▼ 18.7 The greenhouse effect

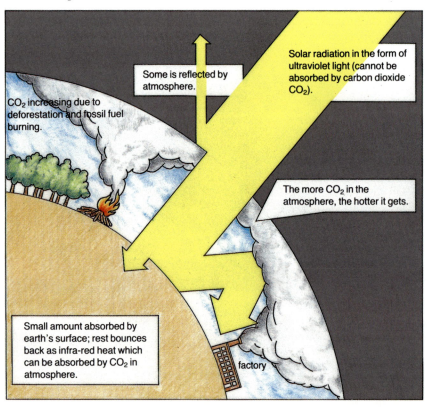

▼ 18.8 The build-up of carbon dioxide

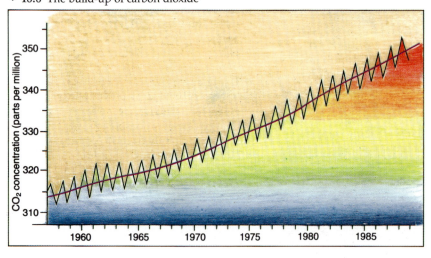

Greenhouse Effect

Although we do not yet fully understand the patterns of, or reasons for, changes in the earth's climate, there is increasing evidence that the earth is heating up. 18.6 shows how temperatures have risen since 1880, the increase during the 1980s being particularly clear.

Heat is held within the atmosphere by a layer of clouds and gases which acts rather like a glass roof 15–25 km above our heads. Gases now being produced on earth and sent into the air are thickening this 'roof', causing a **greenhouse effect**. This means that more of the heat rising from the earth is reflected back to the earth's surface instead of escaping into space (18.7).

There is a range of greenhouse gases.

- **Carbon dioxide** makes up 49% of the total build-up of greenhouse gases. 18.8 shows the rapid increase in carbon dioxide in the air, now estimated to be over 5 billion tonnes per year. This is largely caused by burning fossil fuels. The problem is made worse by the destruction of vast areas of rainforest trees which normally absorb carbon dioxide. Since the trees are often destroyed by burning, releasing even more carbon dioxide, the problem is twice as great.
- **Methane** makes up 18% of greenhouse gases. It is released from animal dung, agriculture, drained or cut peat bogs, and rubbish dumps.
- **Chlorofluorocarbons** (CFCs) make up 14% (but their effect is more concentrated than carbon dioxide). They are found in aerosols, refrigerant and blown-foam packaging.
- **Oxides of nitrogen** make up 6%. These are produced from car exhausts, power stations and nitrogen fertilisers (which are dissolved by rain and eventually evaporate into the atmosphere).
- **Others** make up 13%. Another 36 greenhouse gases are known, many of them used in making and using everyday items such as dry-cleaning solvents. Some scientists fear that many others are still to be discovered.

We know that we are changing the chemical composition of the atmosphere, and that this causes global warming. However, we do not know exactly what will result. As world temperatures rise, ice at the poles will melt and sea levels will rise. But by how much? 18.9 shows one forecast of some of the effects on Britain by 2050.

Global warming will lead to climatic changes in all parts of the world. Precipitation patterns will change, deserts will move, agricultural methods will have to change and whole ecosystems may collapse. It is likely that there will be an increase in extreme weather, with droughts, hurricanes and floods being more common.

Ozone Hole

The ozone layer lies 20–25 km above the earth's atmosphere. It filters out certain harmful types of the sun's rays, particularly ultraviolet radiation. Since the 1960s ozone levels over parts of Antarctica have dropped by almost 40% during some months. Holes are now clearly visible in satellite observations of ozone concentration over both the Antarctic and Arctic. The ozone layer is also shrinking in other parts of the world, for example by about 5% each winter over the UK.

As the ozone layer shrinks, there will be an increase in skin cancers, because more solar radiation will pass through to the earth's surface. 18.10 shows estimates of the possible effects.

Although scientists believe that there could be some natural explanation for the decrease in ozone, there is a growing acceptance that pollution is a major cause. Chiefly to blame are chlorofluorocarbons (CFCs). When they come into contact with ultraviolet radiation they release chlorine into the upper atmosphere. Each chlorine atom may destroy 100 000 ozone molecules. It is thought that nitrous oxide and methane also disrupt the ozone layer.

Immediate action is needed to prevent even more damage being done to the earth by the greenhouse effect and the destruction of ozone. Some of the most important measures are listed below.

- Destruction of the world's forests must cease, and a massive tree-planting programme is needed. Trees absorb vast quantities of carbon dioxide.
- The burning of fossil fuels must be reduced, both by energy conservation and the development of safer fuels. Where fossil fuels are burnt, effective filters must be used to prevent polluting gases from escaping into the atmosphere.
- We must all avoid using potentially polluting chemicals in our homes and gardens. Where possible we should buy food and other goods produced by non-polluting methods, to put pressure on farmers and industry to be more environmentally friendly.
- The production of CFCs should cease, as safer alternatives are now available.

What other action would you suggest? What can individuals do to help?

▲ 18.9 Ark map of Britain, 2050

▼ 18.10 The hole in the sky

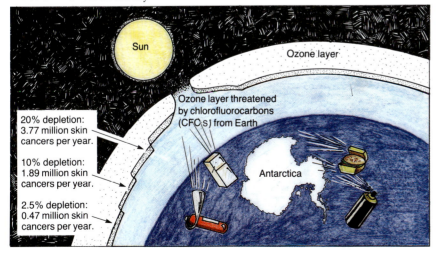

Environmental Decisions 85

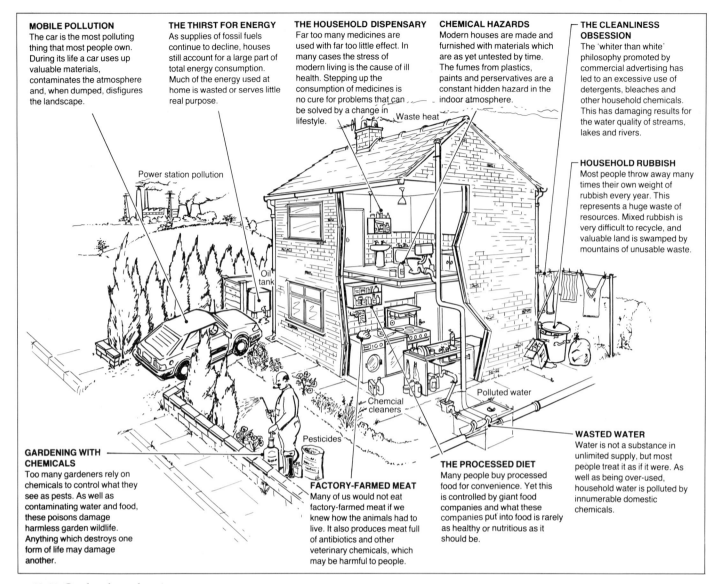

▲ 18.11 Careless housekeeping

Careless Housekeeping

Blame for polluting the earth does not rest solely with factory owners, farmers and the government. While we may feel that all of these are major contributors, it is ordinary householders who continue to demand certain products, and therefore bear an equal or greater responsibility for the pollution that threatens to ruin our planet. You are a member of a household, and you can make decisions that can reduce environmental damage. You can also try to persuade your friends and others in your household to do what they can.

18.11 shows a number of ways in which many individuals are damaging the environment. *Which ones apply to you and your household?*

Action that you can take

In their book *Blueprint for a Green Planet* (Dorling Kindersley, 1987), J. Seymour and H. Girardet suggest a four-point plan that we can all follow.

- **Assess the consequences.** Most everyday decisions affect the environment in some way. They may improve it, or make it deteriorate in some way, or in a few cases leave it unchanged. Discovering which category your action falls into before you make a decision is an essential part of conserving the environment.
- **Encourage positive changes.** If an action enhances the environment, recommend it to others wherever possible. Individual action is only effective at changing things if enough individuals pursue it. Be an individual who sets an example by caring for the environment.
- **Avoid causing damage.** Many actions, such as throwing away large amounts of rubbish, wasting water, or using pesticides, fall into the category of avoidable damage to the environment. In nearly all cases this kind of damage can be prevented with a little thought, without any noticeable change in the quality of life.
- **Cut down what cannot be cut out.** Some actions, such as driving a car, are difficult to avoid at times. The best approach in these cases is to take steps to reduce the damage. So car users should make sure that their cars are as pollution free as possible, take public transport whenever they can, and walk on short journeys.

Damaging the Land

Large-scale farming, like any industry, is concerned with producing high yields for high profit. To achieve this, farmers make use of methods and materials which can result in serious short-term, and long-term, damage both to human health and to the environment (18.12).

But are we as householders any better in our own gardens?

- Many endangered plants have been plundered from their natural habitats to adorn our gardens.
- Millions of hectares of land have been stripped of soil to provide us with peat and compost. The wildlife habitats of these areas are completely destroyed.
- Beneficial as well as harmful insects are killed by pesticides that we use, and the natural balance between pests and predators is upset.
- We use massive quantities of polluting chemicals, when natural fertilisers would be as good.
- We burn or throw away much organic matter that could be used to enrich the soil.
- If stocked with native plants and kept free of chemicals, gardens have enormous potential as wildlife refuges. However, most modern gardens drive out the wildlife.

Some commercial, as well as amateur, gardeners who are worried by the effects of modern farming and gardening techniques are turning to organic methods. 18.13 shows the natural fertilisers and pesticides that can be used, while 18.14 lists the principles of organic gardening as drawn up by the International Federation of Organic Agriculture Movements.

Discuss the arguments for and against organic farming.

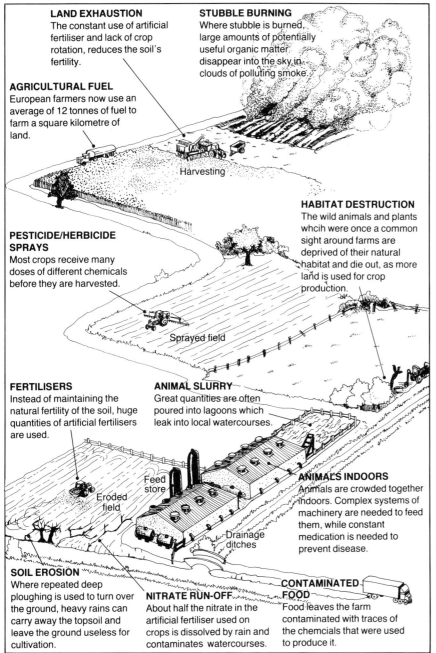

▲ 18.12 How modern farming damages the land

▼ 18.13 Natural fertilisers and pesticides

NATURAL FERTILISERS

- **Animal manure.** This is the most traditional fertiliser of all and needs to be well rotted before it is applied, to prevent it initially robbing the soil of nitrogen.
- **Liquid plant manure.** This can be made by packing the leaves of green manure plants such as comfrey into a water barrel. After a month a highly nutritious (if smelly) liquid is produced.
- **Bonemeal.** This commercial organic fertiliser is rich in phosphate which is released slowly into the soil.
- **Hoof and horn.** Another commercial organic product; it contains as much nitrogen as synthetic fertilisers.
- **Wood ash.** This is the gardener's best source of potash, as effective as mined potash fertilisers.

NATURAL PESTICIDES

- **Soft soap.** This semi-liquid soap kills aphids by dissolving the wax layer on their skins so they die of desiccation.
- **Nicotine.** This *highly poisonous* but natural insecticide kills aphids, scale insects and caterpillars but not ladybirds or hoverflies. It decomposes naturally after use.
- **Quassia.** This is a natural insecticide found in the bark of the tropical quassia tree. The bark is sold in dried form: soaking it produces quassia spray.
- **Potassium soap.** Another harmless aphid control. The soap is dissolved in water and then used as a spray.
- **Derris-pyrethrum.** A plant-produced insecticide which is toxic to nearly all insects – it must be used with care.

▼ 18.14 Principles of organic farming

- **Localism.** As far as possible, an organic farm is run within a closed system, drawing upon local resources instead of relying on raw materials from outside.
- **Soil improvement.** Instead of depleting the soil, the organic farmer aims to maintain and improve its natural fertility. This rules out the use of artificial fertilisers, as these do not improve the soil over the long term.
- **Pollution abatement.** The organic farmer takes steps to avoid all forms of pollution when raising and harvesting crops. This excludes the use of all synthetic pesticides, as these pollute ground, wildlife and food.
- **Quality of produce.** As well as producing food in quantity, the organic farmer places an emphasis on a high nutritional quality in the farm's output.
- **Energy use.** On an organic farm, the use of fossil fuels such as oil is kept to a minimum.

Environmental Decisions

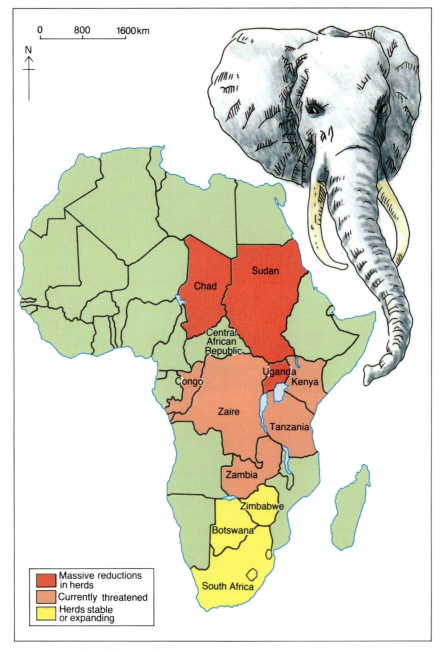

▲ 18.15 Decline of the elephants

▼ 18.16 Ivory carving

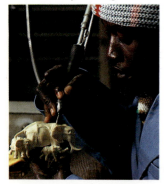

Wildlife at Risk

500 years ago 10 million elephants lived in Africa's forests and savannas. Today the elephant population is less than 700 000, and may soon drop to half a million. It is severely threatened in many areas (18.15).

Individual populations are in a critical position. Kenya and Uganda lost 85% of their elephants between 1973 and 1988. Between 1978 and 1988 the number of elephants in Tanzania's Selous, one of Africa's largest game reserves, was reduced by half. Figures for West and Central Africa paint an equally bleak picture. Even though the sale of ivory is now banned in many countries, measures must be taken to protect this magnificent animal, if the species is to survive. There are a variety of reasons for the decline in elephant numbers.

- The major short-term cause of the alarming decline is *poaching*, to supply the international trade with ivory from elephant tusks. A poacher may well receive several hundred dollars, equal to the average annual income in many African countries, by killing a single elephant. As herds decline, younger elephants with smaller tusks are killed, so more tusks are needed to make up the same weight of ivory; and the demand for ivory trinkets is immense (18.16).
- Occupation of traditional elephant habitats by rapidly growing human populations in many African countries is another important reason for their long-term decline. When Africa had 10 million elephants, only 16 million people lived there. Today the human population has reached 500 million, and the elephants' range has been reduced to less than one-quarter of the continent's surface.
- Some elephants die because of droughts. In Kenya's Tsava National Park over half of its elephants were lost during a five-year drought in the first half of the 1970s.
- Culling operations to maintain populations at manageable levels, including hunting for meat or trophies, occurs in some areas. In Zimbabwe, elephant numbers are rising and, without hunting and culling, elephants would take over farmland and trample entire villages underfoot. But, here, every part of the elephant is sold. The meat is eaten, skins go towards making shoes and handbags, the feet make umbrella stands and the tusks make jewels and ornaments. The business keeps millions from starving and pays for schools and hospitals. A large slice of the cost also goes into protecting the elephant and other animals from poachers.

The experience of Zimbabwe suggests that **controlled** culling and selling of ivory may provide the cash to save the elephant from extinction in the long term. The real need is to control illegal and uncontrolled killing.

The elephant is sadly only one example of wildlife put at risk by human activities. Some 120 other species of mammal are in great danger of becoming extinct, including the polar bear, tiger and rhinoceros. Over 500 000 parrots are traded each year, many from the 30 endangered species. All species of the great apes face extinction in the wild. Throughout the world, wildlife is at risk, and despite the efforts of the conservation groups much still remains to be done to stop the slaughter.

▲ 18.17 Antarctica: the lost wilderness

Antarctica

Antarctica is one of the last relatively untouched wildernesses on earth (18.17). Some people believe that the way we treat it will show whether we really do care about our environment and fellow creatures.

The continent of Antarctica is around 14 million km², about the size of Mexico and the USA put together, and nearly 60 times bigger than the UK. Most of the land is covered in ice, which has an average thickness of 1600 m. Although pack ice is present in the sea around Antarctica all year round, in winter the ice expands to cover 200 million km², and prevents access to those parts of the coast which are normally accessible in the summer months.

It is a very harsh environment, temperatures inland averaging −30 °C in summer and −55 °C in winter, with winds up to 150 km/h. As a result few land species of animals can survive. However, the marine ecosystem is more complex, with large populations of whales, seals, penguins and other aquatic life. They rely on a few basic food sources. If they disappear, the entire ecosystem could collapse.

So far, Antarctica is one of the few places on the earth where international cooperation has worked, for the most part. However, the possible presence of oil and other resources makes the future of the continent less certain.

In 1961 the Antarctic Treaty was signed, which dedicated the continent to peaceful scientific research. There are 18 nations who make decisions jointly (18.18). However, the treaty did not cover the exploitation of wildlife in the surrounding seas. Antarctic whales have been hunted to near extinction, some species only having a slim chance of survival. Commercial cod fishing was banned in 1985 only after stocks became dangerously low. There are now fears that stocks of krill will be decimated with disastrous results, as krill is the mainstay of the food chain.

Only 2% of the continent is ice free, but the human impact on this area is already very marked. Many wildlife colonies and traditional breeding grounds are concentrated on this same area, and have been badly disturbed by human development. With the continual expansion of bases, disturbance is constantly increasing.

The present damage to wildlife could appear insignificant in comparison with the damage caused if exploitation of the vast range of minerals in the area is allowed. It is estimated that in the surrounding seas there are large quantities of oil, while on land there are large deposits of coal and oil (18.18). Conservationists particularly fear an oil spill. Pack ice, hurricane-force winds and icebergs present an untested hazard to drilling rigs and oil tankers. An oil spill would be worse here than anywhere else in the world. A clean-up would be impossible for most of the year because of the intense cold. Similarly, oil would break down 100 times slower than in warmer waters, and could remain a danger to wildlife for many years. The unique Antarctic wildlife would be disastrously affected since nearly all animals live near the sea. Even with no spills, further precious onshore space would be needed for the mining operations, with increased damage to wildlife.

Greenpeace, a conservation group, feels that Antarctica should be preserved as a World Park, and no mineral exploitation allowed. *What do you think?*

▼ 18.18 Antarctica

Antarctic Treaty Decision-Making Nations

Argentina	New Zealand
Australia	Norway
Belgium	Poland
Brazil	South Africa
Chile	UK
China	Uruguay
France	USA
India	USSR
Japan	West Germany

Environmental Decisions

19 Who Cares?

Key ideas
- Many different groups of people are showing increasing concern about the environment.
- Individuals can take action to care for the environment.

We know that human activity is damaging the natural environment in many different ways. In developed areas of the world groups of people have formed **pressure groups** to try to reduce this damage in both developed and developing areas. Two of the best-known pressure groups are Greenpeace and Friends of the Earth (19.1).

In the UK the Green Party is a political pressure group demanding an environmentally friendly attitude to all aspects of managing the country. Support for the Greens grew rapidly in the late 1980s and, although they had no candidates elected to Parliament, their pressure and popularity encouraged the two main parties (Conservative and Labour) to modify some of their ideas and take environmental issues more seriously.

▼ 19.1

Greenpeace
30–31 Islington Green
LONDON N1 8XE

HELP THE EARTH FIGHT BACK

The Earth needs all the friends it can get. And it needs them now. For thousands upon thousands of years, our planet has sustained a wonderfully rich tapestry of life. Now, one single species – humankind – is putting the Earth at risk.

People the world over are suffering the effects of pollution, deforestation and radiation. Species are disappearing at a terrifying rate. The warming of the atmosphere threatens us all with devastating changes in climate and food production.

It needn't be like this. We know enough to reverse the damage, and to manage the Earth's astonishing wealth more fairly and sustainably. But the political will to bring about such a transformation is still lacking.

And that's exactly where Friends of the Earth comes in. Isn't it time you joined us?

A Record of Success Since 1971, Friends of the Earth has led the way in the struggle to protect the environment.

Our wildlife campaigns in the 1970s resulted in bans on the sale of furs from endangered tigers, cheetahs and leopards. It was Friends of the Earth who promoted the 1976 Endangered Species Act, and who forced through a European-wide ban on the sale of all whale products in 1982.

Over the years, our Countryside Campaign has successfully protected many threatened wildlife habitats like ancient woodlands and flower-rich meadows.

In the last couple of years, successful campaigning by Friends of the Earth has:

- persuaded the aerosol and fast-food packaging industries to stop using ozone-destroying CFC chemicals;
- obliged the Government to enforce European laws on drinking water quality and transboundary shipments of toxic wastes;
- forced the Government to tighten controls over the use of pesticides and nitrates;
- convinced the World Bank and British commercial banks to stop funding certain destructive development schemes in the rainforests;
- convinced Coca Cola Co. to pull out of clearing tropical forests in Belize, and to conserve them instead;
- advised the Government of Nigeria (at their invitation) on the safe disposal of 3,800 tonnes of illegally-dumped toxic wastes;
- repeatedly exposed dangerous radiation levels around nuclear power plants and successfully lobbied the UKs National Radiological Protection Board to recommend lower dose limits for workers and the public.

Printed on straw-based paper.
Friends of the Earth
26–28 Underwood Street,
LONDON N1 7JQ

Friends of the Earth

WHAT CAN YOU DO?

Many of the actions that scientists say are needed to improve the environment can be implemented only by large industries and governments but every one of us must play a part, too.

* Choose cruelty-free Sainsbury's cosmetics and toiletries
* Either buy alternatives to aerosols – such as stick or roll-on deodorants – or change to CFC-free aerosols
* Use recycled stationery
* Use phosphate-free detergent
* Recycle glass by using the bottle banks in larger Sainsbury's
* Buy mercury-free batteries
* Burn smokeless fuels
* Be economical with all energy
* Buy unleaded petrol, if your car will take it. If it won't, you can probably get it converted
* Press the local authorities to provide a 'safe' way of disposing of old domestic refrigerators
* Parents of babies and toddlers should choose disposable nappies made without chlorine bleaches
* Choose low-dioxin paper and sanitary products such as those in Sainsbury's
* Buy organic fruits and vegetables

Look out for this shelf label sign on all the environment-friendly products in Sainsbury's.

FRIENDS OF THE EARTH MESSAGE
Friends of the Earth wish Sainsbury's and their customers all the best in their efforts to protect the environment.
There is no doubt that 'green' retailers and consumers can make a difference.

▲ 19.2
▼ 19.3

Consumer Pressure

Consumer pressure in Britain is also having a significant impact on what shops (especially supermarkets) sell. The buyers for the big retailing groups such as Sainsburys (19.2) now prefer environmentally friendly products, and manufacturers are being forced to change their methods of production and packaging. Ozone friendly aerosols and unleaded petrol have been the subject of high-profile advertising campaigns. The issues of plastic packaging (should plastics be used and, if they are, should they be biodegradable or recyclable?) and detergents are also coming increasingly under the spotlight.

Many large companies are sponsoring environmental groups (19.3) to improve their image. For example, in 1985 the World Wide Fund for Nature had an annual sponsorship income of £250 000; in 1989 it was £2.5 million; and for the early 1990s contracts worth £7–8 million have been signed with sponsors.

Many manufacturers in the UK are hoping to expand sales as a result of the European single market in 1992. They are aware that they will have to adopt a more environmentally friendly attitude, as the 'green' consumers in countries such as West Germany and the Netherlands are already a much stronger force than their supporters in the UK.

Discuss the effectiveness of the advertisements shown on pages 90 and 91.

Deep in the heart of Northumberland, there lies an area of land which, after years of yielding to the unrelenting demands of industry, is now lying scarred and desolate.

With your help, we aim to change all that.

The British Trust for Conservation Volunteers is the largest organisation of its kind, involving people of all ages in practical and useful conservation work.

For some years now, BTCV has been generously supported in its work by Prudential Corporation.

We'll turn the pot holes into fox holes and we'll replace the coal tips with cowslips, giving back to nature what nature deserves.

We'll organise enthusiastic people (like yourself, maybe?) who will lovingly restore it to its original, natural splendour.

Each year, over 50 000 volunteers from all walks of life carry out extremely enjoyable and gratifying conservation work on over 15 000 sites throughout the United Kingdom.

We can't promise the earth – but we do promise you a small portion to look after.

Right now it's a deserted coalfield. Soon, with your help, it will be a nature reserve.

PRESERVE YOUR HERITAGE · CONSERVE YOUR LAND · RESERVE YOUR PLACE

PRUDENTIAL *Sponsorship*

Who Cares?

Who Cares? You Do!

In the summer of 1989 a major piece of research was carried out into public concerns, knowledge, and personal action being taken, on a range of environmental issues. Over 47 000 *Radio Times* readers completed a 'Green Questionnaire' designed with the help of the market research company National Opinion Polls (NOP). 19.4 shows some of the results. Nuclear waste emerged as the greatest single pollution concern. An encouraging feature was that the results demonstrated that people were not only concerned about environmental issues but were prepared to do something about them (see details of packaging/waste on 19.4). As with all polls, it was essential to find out whether the people who replied to the questionnaire were an average cross-section of the public. NOP took care to ask certain additional questions which would establish how representative the sample was. It was found that the 47 000 people who replied were *not* representative: 52% of the replies came from people who belonged to an environmental pressure group such as Greenpeace (see pages 90–1) whereas among the British population as a whole this figure is only 12%. Nevertheless, the results are very significant in showing a rising public concern about the environment which is also reflected in a massive growth in membership of environmental pressure groups. In the late 1980s Greenpeace doubled its membership in two years while Friends of the Earth grew by 150% in 18 months.

▼ 19.4 Survey results, *Radio Times*, 3–9 June 1989

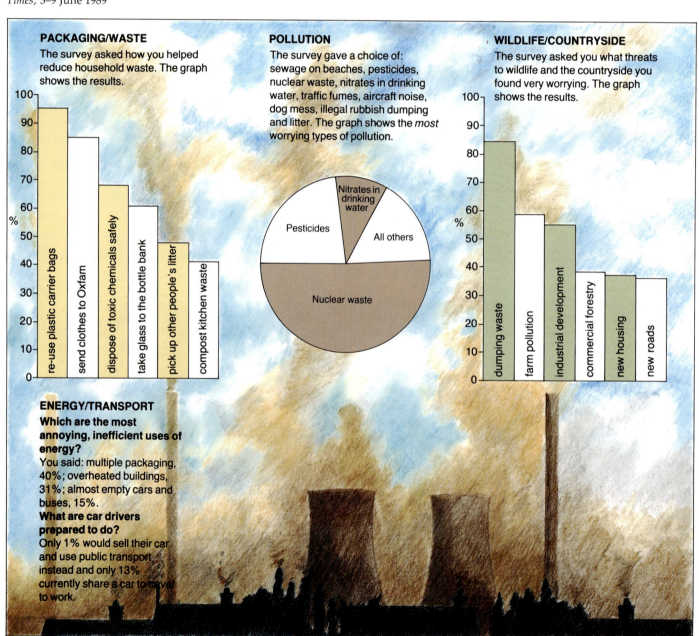

What do you care about most?

Look again at the sort of information collected in 19.4. Work in groups to design a questionnaire to collect information about people's attitudes towards environmental issues. Try to include questions which:

- ask about environmentally friendly products used or not used;
- ask for a list of given issues to be put into rank order of importance;
- ask about issues in the developing world;
- ask about any local issues such as pollution of a local river.

If you cannot think of issues to ask questions about, then have a look through this textbook!

Having decided what questions you want to ask, make sure you give the questionnaire to different groups of people, to compare their attitudes. You might sample

- different age groups;
- males and females;
- people who live in different areas of a city, or who live in a rural area.

When you have collected your results, produce graphs to analyse your data and write about your conclusions.

The Netherlands: the Cost of Turning Green

The Netherlands is one of the most densely populated countries in the world. It has led the way in the EC in taking measures against pollution. The threats are many and complex (19.5) but the government has produced an action plan to reduce pollution by 70–90% by 2010, and to reduce energy use by 30% in the same period. Opinion polls show that more than 90% of the Dutch people are prepared to accept lower living standards for the sake of a cleaner country, and 50% said they would be prepared to have the use of their car restricted to aid a healthier environment. Because much of the Netherlands is at or below sea level, people feel particularly at risk from global warming and the rise in sea level that may follow.

The plan includes action on controlling car exhaust emission, reducing sulphur dioxide output, and fines for illegal dumping of heavy metals.

The plan is based on the principle of 'the polluter pays' and some industrialists have warned that higher environmental standards will make them less competitive. It remains to be seen whether opposing groups will emerge who are not prepared to pay the price of a cleaner and healthier environment.

Organise a discussion where the advantages and disadvantages of the principle 'the polluter pays' are brought out. Look at the various arguments from the points of view of an individual, a manufacturing company, and the government.

▼ 19.5 Netherlands national environment plan

Netherlands national environment plan
Aim: cut pollution 70–90% by 2010
Cost: $3bn, based on the principle of polluter pays

Who Cares? 93

Glossary

Terms have been explained here if they are important or if they were not described fully in the main text.

Abstraction. A general term for taking water from a store in the hydrological cycle such as a surface lake or ground water.
Afforestation. Planting land with trees for commercial or amenity value.
Amenity. A natural or non-natural feature connected with human leisure use.
Aquifer. A layer of rock which holds water and allows water to pass through it. Water can be abstracted from an aquifer for use.
Artesian water. Water in an aquifer (sandwiched between impermeable rock layers) which flows to the surface under its own pressure. It may do this naturally or as a result of a well being sunk.
Balance of trade. The difference between the value of a country's imports and exports.
Base load. The basic supply of electricity (and other resources) needed to meet demand at non-peak times.
Biomass. The weight of vegetation in a fixed area, measured in dry kilograms per square metre. Areas of tropical rainforest have very high biomass figures.
Cash crop. A crop grown for sale rather than one grown for use by the farmer or the farmer's family.
Catchment area. The area over which precipitation falls and is caught to feed into a single natural drainage basin.
Conservation. Positive action to protect such things as natural resources, wildlife, soil, etc. for present and future generations.
Deforestation. The loss or deliberate removal of forest.
Deposition. The laying down of material which has been moved by an agent of erosion such as a glacier, a river or the sea.
Drainage basin. An area of land with a common outlet for its surface water which is drained by a single river system.
Ecosystem. The living things (animals and plants) of a particular area and the way they interact with each other and with the physical and chemical environment in which they live.
Energy supplies. A general term to include both **primary** supplies such as coal and crude oil and **secondary** supplies such as electricity made from a primary supply.
Environmentally friendly (substance, process or attitude). One which results in less damage to the environment.

Erosion. The wearing away of the land surface by a variety of agents, the most important of which are rivers, the sea, glaciers, and wind.
Eutrophication. Excess growth of plants and animals in rivers, lakes and coastal areas caused by large amounts of food such as nitrates entering the water due to human activity.
Exploitation. Making use of a resource. Sometimes used to suggest the resource is being used at an excessive or unacceptable rate.
Finite. Having an end or limit. Used to describe resources of which there is a fixed amount; i.e. once used up, they cannot be replaced (e.g. coal). Non-finite (renewable) resources (e.g. forest) can be replaced.
Fossil fuels. Fuels formed millions of years ago from the remains of plants and animals: e.g. coal, crude oil, natural gas. They are finite (non-renewable) resources.
Geothermal energy. Heat and power obtained from hot rocks at varying depths below the earth's surface.
Global warming. The theory that the earth's climate is getting warmer due mainly to a build-up of carbon dioxide in the atmosphere. Also called the **greenhouse effect**, so called because carbon dioxide and other greenhouse gases keep the earth warmer by preventing the escape of heat that would normally be lost from the atmosphere.
Habitat. A place with the kind of environmental conditions in which a particular plant or animal usually lives.
Humus. Part of soil made from decomposed animal and plant matter. It is usually dark coloured and helps to retain moisture.
Hydro-electric power (HEP). Electricity generated using a natural or artificial head (fall) of water.
Hydrograph. A record (graph) of the amount of water flowing in a river or stream over a fixed period of time.
Hydrological cycle. The natural cycle in which water continually circulates between land, air and ocean.
Impermeable. Rock or soil that does not let water pass through it.
Infant mortality rate. The number of infants under 1 year old who die each year out of each 1000 babies born alive.
Irrigation. Watering the land to enable crops to grow in areas where rainfall alone would not be enough to keep them alive or

to allow yields to be as high as farmers desire.

Landfill. The dumping of wastes of various kinds in holes in the ground. The holes may be natural or result from human activities such as quarrying.

Mechanisation. The use of machines to do work previously done by humans. Mechanisation may cause problems of unemployment.

Mining. The general name for a range of processes by which (mainly finite) raw materials are taken from the surface or near surface of the earth.

Nature reserve. An area where the animals and/or plants are protected from damage. Human access may be banned or restricted.

Nomads. People who constantly move from one area to another often using regular routes. The movement is related to the search for food; especially food for grazing animals.

Overfishing. Taking so many fish from an area of water that the overall stock is reduced and catches start to decline.

Overgrazing. Keeping so many animals on an area of grassland that the quality of grazing falls and in time the grass itself may die.

Pollution. Damage to the environment as a result of human activity. Often the complicated nature of the damage is not easily seen or fully understood.

Pressure group. A group of people who share a particular viewpoint on certain issues and who try to bring about change by influencing government and public opinion.

Raw material. Basic material (e.g. iron ore, cotton, wood), natural or partly produced, which is changed by industrial or manufacturing process into a product which is then used.

Reclamation (land). The recovering or improvement of land so that it can be made useful. Usually applied to land which has become derelict after industrial activity.

Recycling. Using manufactured products to make new and useful products. Usually applied to materials (e.g. glass, paper) which after processing can be used again. Recycling is especially important as it avoids using up finite raw materials.

Reserves. The amount of a resource that can be exploited economically at current levels of technical skill.

Rubbish. A general name for waste. Much rubbish is not waste at all but can be re-used, recycled or reprocessed for further use.

Shanty town. An area of very poor-quality housing and very few services found mainly around the edges of urban areas in the developing world.

Siltation. The deposition of silt carried by a river in a lake or the sea. Artificial reservoirs often trap large amounts of silt which reduces the storage capacity of the reservoir.

Soil erosion. The wearing away and loss of topsoil mainly due to wind, rain and running water.

Soil profile. A vertical slice through soil which shows the different layers (or horizons).

Succession. The progressive natural development of vegetation that takes place in one area over a long period of time. Simple plants like lichens are replaced by a series of increasingly complex plants until the most advanced plants that can be supported in the area develop.

Trophic levels. Levels within a food chain in an ecosystem. The basic one is the producer trophic level (plants) which supports higher levels of consumers (animals).

Water surplus. When the availability of water in an area is greater than the demand. A water **deficit** is where the demand for water in an area exceeds the supply.

Weathering. The physical, chemical and biological processes (mainly associated with weather) which cause rocks to weaken, break down or disintegrate without being removed. The weathered **debris** may later be eroded.

Index

abrasion 38
acid rain 56, 82, 83
acquicludes 9
adit mine 59
aeration 18
afforestation 32
agro-forestry 31
algal blooms 19
alternative energy 72–7
Antarctic Treaty 89
anthracite 58
aquaculture 79
aqueducts 16–17, 21
aquifers 9, 12
arches 38
artesian bore holes 9
attrition 38

backwash 37
bar 36
base load power station 57
beaches 36–9, 81
biochemical oxygen demand (BOD) 18
biogas digester 19, 76
biomass 23, 28, 54, 76
biomass fuels 54, 76
bio-reactor 50
biosphere reserve 41
birth control 30
bituminous coal 58
bore hole 9, 12–13
bottle banks 53
broadleaf forests 28–9, 33
brown earth soil 24
buildings (corrosion of) 83

cancer 87
canopy 29
carbon dioxide 84
car exhausts 82–3
carnivores 23
cash crops 35
China syndrome 71
chlorofluorocarbons (CFCs) 85
cholera 10
clay 24, 46
cliffs 36–9
climatic change 4–5, 30, 34–5, 84–5, 92–3
climax vegetation 23
coal 54–61, 89
coal measures 59
coal reserves 58
coal seams 59
coal trade 58
coastal erosion 38
coastal protection 38
coasts 36–9
coking coal 58
common fisheries policy 79
concealed coalfield 61
coniferous forest 22, 28–9, 32
conservation 41, 78–9, 86–7
continental shelf 79
contour ploughing 26

country park 42–3, 46–7
culling 88

dams 7–9, 14–15, 21, 73
deciduous woodland 33
decomposers 23–4
deforestation 15, 30–1, 32–3, 84
demersal fish 78
deposition 36–9
dereliction 42–5
desalination 17, 78
desertification 4–5, 12, 34–5
deserts 4–5, 27, 34–5
diarrhoea 10
drainage basin 7
drainage schemes 40
drift mine 59
drinking water 8–19, 21
drought 34–5
drugs 30
dunes 36–9
dust 46
dysentery 10, 30

ecological niche 23
ecosystem 22–3, 36–41
electricity 56–7
electric transmission lines 56–7
electromagnetic radiation 56
elephant 88
emergents 29
endangered species 81, 88
energy 54–77
    conservation 77
    consumption 55
environmental care 86–7
environmental groups 90–3
environmentally friendly products 90–1
erosion 36–9
estuary 36–7
ethanol 5
eutrophication 19
evaporation 7
exposed coalfield 61
extinction (of plants and animals) 4–5, 36–9, 40–1, 78–89
eye diseases 10

factory fishing 78
fallow 24, 35
farming 4–5, 86–7
fast-breeder reactor 68
fertiliser 26–7, 87
fisheries 78–9, 89
fish farming 79
fish quotas 79
food chain 22
food web 23
forests 4–5, 22, 28–33, 42, 83, 85
fossil fuels 54, 67
fractionating tower 66
Friends of the Earth 90

gas coal 58

gas turbine 56–7
geothermal energy 54, 75
glass 53
glaucoma 30
global warming 84
grassland 22
gravel 5, 46
greenhouse effect 84
Greenpeace 90
ground water 7, 9, 15, 17, 83
groynes 36
gully erosion 25

hardwoods 29
head of water 72
hedgerows 23, 26
herbivores 23
hookworm 10
horizons (in soil) 24
hot desert 22
humus 24
hydraulic action 38
hydro-electric power 9, 14–15, 54–7, 72
hydrograph 9
hydrological cycle 7

impermeable 9
incineration 48
infiltration 7
interception 7
irrigation 14–15, 16–17, 35, 79
ivory 88

lagoons 36–7
lakes 4–5, 14, 40–1, 83
landfill 42–3, 46, 48–51
landfill gas 50–1
land management 42–5
leaching 24
leprosy 58
lignite 58
longshore drift 36–7

malaria 10, 30
marina 36
marram grass 37
marshland 36–7, 40–1
medicines 30
merry-go-round 56
metal ores 5
metals 52
methane 84
minerals 24
mountains 4–5
mudflats 36–7

National Grid 57
National Parks 31–2, 42
National Rivers Authority 18
natural gas 54–6, 62–7
navigation (water-borne) 14–15
nitrates 19
nitrogen oxides 56, 82–3
noise pollution 46